Reading Pope's
Imitations of Horace

Reading Pope's
Imitations of Horace

Jacob Fuchs

Lewisburg
Bucknell University Press
London and Toronto: Associated University Presses

Associated University Presses
440 Forsgate Drive
Cranbury, NJ 08512

Associated University Presses
25 Sicilian Avenue
London WC1A 2QH, England

Associated University Presses
P.O. Box 488, Port Credit
Mississauga, Ontario
Canada L5G 4M2

The paper used in this publication meets the requirements
of the American National Standard for Permanence of Paper
for Printed Library Materials Z39.48-1984.

Library of Congress Cataloging-in-Publication Data

Fuchs, Jacob.
  Reading Pope's imitations of Horace.

  Bibliography: p.
  Includes index.
  1. Pope, Alexander, 1688–1744. Imitations of Horace.
2. Horace—Parodies, imitations, etc. 3. Horace—
Influence—Pope. 4. English poetry—Roman influences.
5. Imitation (in literature) I. Title.
PR3630.I53F84 1989   821'.5   87-46437
ISBN 0-8387-5148-2 (alk. paper)

PRINTED IN THE UNITED STATES OF AMERICA

FOR FREYA

Contents

Preface 9
Acknowledgments 11

1 Reading the Imitation 15
2 Augustus 28
3 Horace 42
4 Reading Horace 53
5 Beginning 63
  The First Satire of the Second Book of Horace Imitated 63
6 Extremes: Ofellus and the Rake 77
  The Second Satire of the Second Book of Horace
   Paraphrased 77
  Sober Advice from Horace 85
7 Refuge in a Toppling World 93
  An Epistle to Dr. Arbuthnot 93
  The Second Epistle of the Second Book of Horace,
   Imitated 97
8 Confronting the Age 112
  The First Epistle of the Second Book of Horace,
   Imitated 112
9 Toward Silence 124
  The Sixth Epistle of the First Book of Horace Imitated 124
  The First Epistle of the First Book of Horace Imitated 128

Appendix. *Epilogue to the Satires:* Farewell to Horace 143
Notes 146
Select Bibliography 159
Index 165

Preface

Many years ago I discovered in myself a liking for both Horace and Pope and therefore began to think of the latter's *Imitations of Horace* as a subject for a book. Luckily, circumstances led me to delay the writing of this book, until I had prepared and published another one, a translation of Horace's *sermones,* the satires and epistles from which Pope selected the poems he imitated.

Translators are not imitators, as the first chapter of this book points out. But both begin with the same experience, which is basically one of comparing. Like Pope, then, I looked through the window of Horace's hexameters into a civilization ancestral to my own and both like it and unlike it in equally fascinating ways. Although my work, as translation, proceeded in a different way from Pope's imitations, it gave me a sense of connectedness with Horace's Rome. It prepared me, when I turned again to the *Imitations,* to notice and to be particularly impressed not by the similarities but by the differences between Augustan Rome and contemporary England that Pope observed and from which, as I seek to show, he created meaning in these poems.

Pope will speak to us most meaningfully, of course, on concerns that matter greatly both to himself and to us. The first four chapters of this book will demonstrate that neither the supposed limitations of the imitation form nor eighteenth-century attitudes regarding Horace and Augustus prevented the poet from expressing himself on such concerns. Chapters 5 through 9 are then devoted to interpretation of the *Imitations,* which reveal Pope constantly making variations on Horace. These lead him to explore and discard a series of satiric stances and strategies as he moves toward impasse. My subject is his progress toward this point.

Acknowledgments

I am indebted to California State University, Hayward for grants that allowed me time for work on this book and to La Sainte Union College, Southampton, for assistance rendered me in the preparation of the last of its several versions. Thanks are also due to the editors of *Classical and Modern Literature* for permission to reprint material in chapter 8 that appeared, in somewhat altered form, in their publication and to W. W. Norton and Company for permission to quote throughout from my translation, *Horace's Satires and Epistles.*

It is my pleasure here to thank those who read my manuscript at various stages and offered both heartening encouragement and significant help: John Traugott, Martin B. Friedman, and Frederick Crews.

Reading Pope's
Imitations of Horace

1

Reading the Imitation

To many the imitation has seemed a slender, unsatisfactory vehicle for meaning. Perhaps the most militant statement of objections to the form appears in Samuel Johnson's *Life of Pope,* in regard to the *Imitations of Horace:*

> The *Imitations of Horace* seem to have been written as relaxations of his genius. This employment became his favourite by its facility; the plan was ready to his hand, and nothing was required but to accommodate as he could the sentiments of an old author to recent facts or familiar images; but what is easy is seldom excellent: such imitations cannot give pleasure to common readers. The man of learning may be sometimes surprised and delighted by an unexpected parallel; but the comparison requires knowledge of the original, which will likewise often detect strained applications. Between Roman images and English manners there will be an irreconcileable dissimilitude, and the work will be generally uncouth and party-coloured; neither original nor translated, neither ancient nor modern.[1]

Thus did Johnson dispose of my subject and, seemingly, of all other imitations. How well can they be defended? I should immediately concede Johnson's objection that the imitation requires of the reader a "knowledge of the original"; without that, the imitation becomes itself an original poem as far as the reader is concerned. By referring to, quoting from, or sometimes printing entire the original texts, writers of imitations did their best to forestall that possibility. But according to Johnson's argument, even the "man of learning" will find in the imitation only scant delight: able to note the occasional "unexpected parallel," he also regards with disapproval the "strained applications" and recognizes the object before him as the verbal equivalent of the hodgepodge painting, "undique collatis membris," with which the oft-imitated Horace begins the *Ars Poetica.* To defend the imitation, one must respond to Johnson's charge that it "will be generally uncouth and party-coloured; neither original nor translated, neither ancient nor modern."

Although it could be claimed that some imitations, like the John Boyle version of Horace to be discussed below, contain few "strained applications," these are not the imitations most worth defending. Taking no risks, they provide parallels that are seldom unexpected and seldom witty. On the other hand, the celebrated imitations of Pope, as well as, I believe, those of Johnson himself, often depart from their Latin models in quite conspicuous ways. This introductory chapter will attempt to explain how the reader responds to these apparent breaches of faith.

It is true that modern critics object less strenuously than Johnson did to the striking contrasts that sometimes appear between an imitation and its source. Some pay little attention to sources, preferring—against the imitators' intentions—to treat imitations as independent poems, while others write of general contrasts, as between Horace's good nature and Pope's spleen, without dwelling much on specifics. Not long ago critics who did consider these particular differences saw them mainly as keys to the imitator's rhetorical strategy, not considering the response of the reader comparing the two poems.[2] Another, more recent, approach seeks to demonstrate that few discrepancies exist: the imitator's source is considered to include not just the poem itself but the Renaissance and post-Renaissance commentary on it.[3]

Practical critics, on the other hand, are often willing to let contrasts remain contrasts and to consider them in interpretation. But although they have taken into account the "strained applications" that Johnson felt could only annoy the reader, they have not made the reader's response to these and to less striking disparities an object of study. (Nor have they focused as consistently upon them as will the present study of the *Imitations of Horace*.) Johnson's criticism remains unanswered, and the imitation imperfectly understood and generally undervalued. By trying to answer Johnson, I hope to revise our definition of the genre, by including the kind of mental activity the imitation leads us to perform, and thus to show its capacity for expressing complex and significant meaning.

Before considering this topic, it should be understood that the imitation is not merely a flawed kind of free translation; for imitations and translations are read in different ways. After clarifying that distinction, this chapter will attempt to support the thesis that the imitation develops much of its meaning through contrasts to the source poem, for these give the reader an opportunity to join in the dialogue of the texts.

Aubrey L. Williams has regretted a general "inclination to value Pope's work [i.e., the *Imitations of Horace*] most highly when it is closest to the original (that is, when it is closest to what can be called a 'spirited translation')" and to value it less when it "varies or departs widely from Horace."[4] This inclination, though mistaken, is quite understandable, since the imitation is closely related, even in its origins, to " 'spirited' " or free translation.

"[I]f *Virgil* must needs speak English," wrote John Denham in 1656, "it were fit he should speak not only as a man of this Nation, but as a man of this age." In 1791, Alexander Tytler also made speaking to the present the essence of good translation, "in which the merit of the original work is so completely transfused into another language as to be as distinctly apprehended, and as strongly felt, as it is by those who speak the language of the original work." Nearly all those concerned with translation who lived between Denham's time and Tytler's agreed. Free translation prevailed, as it prevails today.[5]

Therefore Harold F. Brooks was probably right to conclude that, since free translation "implied the right to modernize settings and allusions," it led to the writing of imitations.[6] But as the quotations from Tytler and Denham suggest, free translation relies heavily on what George Steiner calls translation's "incorporative" movement. To convey the meaning that the source texts have or had in their own languages, translators partly naturalize them, incorporating them within their own "semantic field."[7] In Pope's Homer, for example, the heroes speak and sometimes act like eighteenth-century English noblemen; the translator intended to give his readers the understanding, which he had drawn from the Greek, that Homer's heroic fighters are also noblemen.

A free translation succeeds, obviously, if it says to its readers approximately what the original said to its original readers, the translator having captured its meaning with the materials his own language and culture afford. The goal is to create a self-sufficient work that makes direct knowledge of the source unnecessary for the reader, and any translation that forces a resort to the original is usually regarded as inept. No wonder that free translation has always been favored over literal. But the imitation, despite the form's origin as an outgrowth of free translation, cannot incorporate its source; to be identifiable as an imitation, it must make outright departures: London must replace Rome, for example, or George II replace Augustus. One can detect none of these departures without resorting to the source.

Free translation incorporates; in order to be what it is, the imitation depends on contrast. To Johnson's objection that the imitation is "neither original nor translated," the appropriate response seems to be that, while the text may have stretches of translation in it, we recognize it as an imitation because of its differences from the source. Of course, readers rely on a convention of parallelism. They know that similarities exist between the equivalent persons and places in the two texts. After grasping that Rome and London are both major cities or George and Augustus both rulers, they may note further, more complex similarities or, in some cases, dissimilarities. But the whole process begins with noting a basic unlikeness: Johnson's city in *London* is not Rome; George Augustus, even in the hands of a sycophantic imitator who takes the comparison seriously, is not Augustus Caesar.

One knows this at the beginning, when first meeting the equivalents in the imitation, and one knows this at its end. For no matter what the imitator says, readers remain aware of the differences of years and languages and cultures. One poem's world does not take over that of the other; worlds and poems remain apart, juxtaposed in the mind as the texts of original and imitation frequently are to the eye. In reading the imitation one faces a texture of rifts, not the uniform, assimilated texture of the translation.

When one notices a difference, whether simple or complex, between imitation and source, as long as one does not merely object to it as an instance of translation failure, one will probably try to account for it. Each difference, it may be said, poses a question: if London appears in the place of Rome, how is it like Rome? More complex differences, including "strained applications," require more complex answers, and these, as I shall show, contribute substantially to the meaning of the imitation. Thus the reader enters into a dialogue with the texts.

Of course, as Wolfgang Iser has pointed out, something similar occurs when one meets the unexpected in proceeding from one element within a narrative to the next. Although a "gap" might be dismissed as a breakdown in coherence and condemned or ignored, readers may instead "bring into play [their] own faculty for establishing connections—for filling in the gaps [guided by their sense of where the text is headed] left by the text itself."[8] But the imitation's reader must fill gaps not only between the sequential elements of the English text, but also between equivalent elements in the imitation and its source. Although any literary allusion calls for some measure of dialectical referring, the imitation has a single, closely followed text; hence the reader's activity is both more concentrated and more continual than it is even with the most heavily allusive conventional text.

Of course there is not only one reader, and different readers will fill the gaps in differing ways. For the imitation to keep its life, the gaps must be treated as persisting opportunities for dialogue, invitations to participate. However, the imitator has strong controls upon interpretation in the two texts: it is usually clear, at least, at what point one poem is alluding to the other. Let us consider three examples which illustrate how the reader mediates between imitation and source.

One of the most common uses of the imitation was to praise by comparison. Thus John Boyle compares Lord Chesterfield to Maecenas through imitating Horace in *The First Ode of the First Book of Horace Imitated* (Pamphlet, London, 1741). At the conclusion, the flavor of which is typical of the entire short poem, Boyle addresses Chesterfield as his patron:

> If you—shou'd place me with th' immortal Choir
> Of Bards, that whilom struck th' harmonious Lyre;
> With heav'nly Rapture fir'd, sublime I'll rise,
> And Snatch the radiant Glories of the Skies.

> (p. 13)

Boyle has extended but not significantly changed Horace's two-line conclusion: "Quodsi me lyricis vatibus inseres, / sublimi feriam sidera vertice" (35–36). He gives us no reminders of the age in which he writes. But although the reader understands that a certain historical parallel exists between that and the Augustan Age, not even the most doctrinaire "Augustan" could fail to see how different the two ages are in many particulars, certainly including the area of relationships between client and patron. For Chesterfield to get the praise Boyle intended, the gap between him and Maecenas must be filled. Despite the differences, pure excellence remains the same across the ages; so the flattery goes in this imitation, as in many others. Since readers will grasp the point for themselves, perhaps they will be impressed.

But they will see it too easily. The text is blank. Because it lacks details, it fails to place us securely in the age of Boyle and Chesterfield and lets us provide only a simple, general answer, a vague greatness, to the posed question, "Why is this contemporary an equivalent to someone ancient?" In these lines, as in the entire ode, Boyle writes about Chesterfield almost as if he actually were Maecenas. There is a boring shortage of gaps; the reader, faced with what Iser calls "minimal indeterminacy," obliged to look on without acting, will not take a strong interest in the poem.[9]

In contrast, the imitations one reads with interest give their reader much more to do. Rather than virtually ignoring the present, as does Boyle's ode, they place it in the foreground and confront the reader with many gaps, some of the difficult kind Johnson called "strained applications." This is the class into which the next example falls. Its presence can lead us to detect both an interesting complexity and some additional moral weight in the generally mediocre *The State of Rome Under Nero and Domitian: A Satire* (pamphlet, London, 1739), attributed to Paul Whitehead.

It should be said that this poem, which combines imitations of parts of several Latin satires, is a true imitation, even though the names of its places and people are the Latin ones used by Juvenal and Persius. Since it draws upon the innuendo employed by journalists of the opposition to Robert Walpole, one can easily see what English places and people Whitehead means. Thus, in a passage that imitates part of Juvenal's fourth satire, Domitian's minister, Catullus, is obviously Walpole himself. But here, while Whitehead establishes a close equivalency between the two figures, he also sharply diverges from his source.

Like the ancient Catullus, the modern minister is dishonest, ruthless, and lustful. Like Catullus, Walpole is described as blind, probably in reference to his moral vision. However while Juvenal's Catullus is "caecus adulator," a pitiful "blind flatterer" who will praise anyone or anything to keep in favor at court, Walpole receives abundant flattery and passes out favors. He even manipulates a stupid "Prince" who is most unlike the terrifying Domitian. How different from Domitian's feeble courtier is this "great *Catullus*,"

> Whose Levee's [are] daily crowded with Resort
> Of a depending, gaping, servile Court.
> Who grants all Honours of the Sword and Gown,
> Glads with a Nod, and ruins with a Frown,
> Who led his Emp'ror in a String, and sway'd
> That Prince whom once the subject World obey'd.
>
> (p. 14)

No parallel to these lines exists in the Latin on the subservient Catullus. By insisting on the contrast, Whitehead has created a "strained application" that may seem to undermine the equivalence between Walpole and Catullus. However, after the surprise, the reader can fill this gap without much difficulty: as a flattered Catullus, with power added to the vices he shares with his Roman counterpart, Walpole becomes an alarming figure indeed.

Now that I have given a preliminary sense of what I believe happens when an imitation is read, it seems appropriate to deal with two questions. First, should readers consider all differences between imitation and original as opportunities for interpretation? Second, in reading an imitation, how firmly wedded should one be to a strict reconstruction of the imitator's probable understanding of the ancient source poem? Is Howard D. Weinbrot correct in arguing that "the student should attempt to reclaim the contemporary reading"?[10]

In response to the first of these questions, we can certainly say that readers will be interpreting nothing if they try to fill gaps that exist because of the imitator's negligence. Prior, for example, may have merely allowed his poem to fall away from its supposed source in the first seventy-eight lines of his "Satyr on the Poets," an imitation of Juvenal's seventh satire: he attacks bad poets for being stupid enough to imagine they can find a patron, while Juvenal, in the parallel lines (1–35), complains about the stinginess of patrons. Of course we cannot always be sure when the imitator is being negligent, but the usual result will be obscurity, since we lack the guiding direction given by intention. Therefore we will lose interest, for, as Iser notes, not only "boredom" but "overstrain" will make the reader "opt out of the game."[11]

The second objection mentioned above has particular relevance to students of the *Imitations of Horace,* since some modern scholars, headed by Professor Weinbrot, claim that Pope and his contemporaries were scornful of both Augustus and Horace, indeed of the entire Augustan Age.[12] This view seems largely mistaken, as succeeding chapters will explain. But let us assume for a moment proof of the period's and Pope's deep disdain. Let us also assume that I share little or none of it. Should I, in reading the *Imitations,* come to the Horatian source poems prepared to impose on them the same negative values that I think Pope imposed? Probably I should if I want to understand Pope's poems based on them as illustrations of his and his period's views of the Augustan Age. I am not at all sure, however, that I can understand them as literary works if I take this historicist approach.

First, a text can have genuine implications that its author did not foresee, as the leading exponent of intentionalism, E. D. Hirsch, Jr., has reminded us.[13] One should seek to discover what the author meant, but one can unduly limit meaning through being too specific. Second, both the imitation and its source have to be read, and the wisdom of a principle that will allow the latter to be misread is questionable: obviously Horace held favorable views concerning

Augustus and the Augustan Age. A final problem relates to the vigorous, comparing, dialectical role that the imitation leads its readers to play. How can one read in this involved and active way while employing what one takes to be another's perspective?

In any case, an anti-Augustan perspective was not, as I shall show, characteristic of the eighteenth century, and nothing in the preceding paragraphs is meant to suggest that one ought to deny the influence of Pope's period on his poetry and somehow read the *Imitations* as if they had no point of origin. The past is not alien territory. We should neither arrogantly ignore it when examining one of its products nor assume that we should or could ignore our own place in the present in order to understand something created before our time but still alive for us.

Having begun the present chapter with Samuel Johnson and his criticism of the imitation, I think it best to draw from his work for the last and most extended example. (I hope that the reader will accept the possibility of poet and critic differing in the same man and of the poet working intuitively within a form the critic misunderstands and dislikes.) Since, as John Butt once pointed out, both of Johnson's imitations of Juvenal illustrate his lifelong "bent . . . towards generalization,"[14] they allow fewer opportunities to perceive contrasts than do, for example, the more specific imitations of Pope. Even so, the comparing reader will notice contrasts that matter in interpretation, some of them belonging to the class of strained applications.

I have chosen to concentrate on Johnson's treatment of the first vain wish, for gold, in *The Vanity of Human Wishes,* whose source is Juvenal's tenth satire. Although I could as easily have chosen a passage in *London,* modeled on Juvenal's third, the former poem seems to be more of a challenge since it is not often read as an imitation. Johnson's Oxford editors have even attempted to lift it partly out of that evidently inferior category: "Imitation though it is, the freedom and sincerity of the treatment make it an original poem."[15] Even a reader lacking prejudice against the form may fail to see the importance of comparing Juvenal's Latin to Johnson's English, since Johnson had printed only the line numbers of certain passages in the tenth satire, while having lines from the third satire printed with *London.* Finally, it is hard to see how comparisons with Juvenal could add to the grandeur and solemnity of a great moral poem. Nonetheless, without losing their sense of its monumental quality, readers can work through the differences between

The Vanity of Human Wishes and Juvenal's satire to a more refined sense of what Johnson meant.

Critics have, indeed, often recognized one obvious gap that occurs at his poem's conclusion, where, as one of them has said, "Juvenal's half-ironic stoicism is transformed by Johnson into an otherwordly Christian 'consolatio.'"[16] There are no equivalents to "happier Seat" and "Death kind Nature's Signal of Retreat" (363–64) for Juvenal, whose concerns are this life and getting through it. Johnson has strained an application, although this seems to bother no one. The real question about the conclusion, apparently, is, how well does the rest of the poem prepare for it. Most consider it an appropriate ending, but there have always been dissenters, and it has recently again been judged "an inadequate and unsatisfying response."[17]

Although the main purpose of the discussion below is merely to illustrate the process of reading an imitation, some interest may also conceivably lie in its affirmation of the more traditional view. Comparison of Johnson's lines 21–48 to the tenth satire's 12–17 strongly suggests that in the world of the imitation, unlike the juster world of the Latin poem, no one could simply and stoically withstand the effects of the contagion of gold.

After lines 1–20, which parallel Juvenal's 1–11 in a general way, Johnson's note indicates that his 21–44 will cover the same ground as the Latin 12–22; the succeeding note links his 45–48 and Juvenal's 23–27. From 12 through 27 Juvenal scorns gold as an object of desire because it brings trouble to those who have it, trouble spared those who lack it. If one looked only at a paraphrase of the Latin, rather than the text itself, one might believe that Johnson was closely following his model. However, a comparison of the Latin and English passages reveals several significant departures from the source, and these will direct us toward a different understanding of the whole passage: for Johnson, though not for Juvenal, gold is a general plague that the poor almost certainly do not escape.

Since the tenth satire is not customarily printed alongside Johnson's imitation, lines 12–27 in the Loeb edition will be provided here:

> sed plures nimia congesta pecunia cura
> strangulat et cuncta exuperans patrimonia census
> quanto delphinis ballaena Britannica maior.
> temporibus diris igitur iussuque Neronis
> Longinum et magnos Senecae praedivitis hortos

clausit et egregias Lateranorum obsidet aedes
tota cohors: rarus venit in cenacula miles.
pauca licet portes argenti vascula puri
nocte iter ingressus, gladium contumque timebis
et motae ad lunam trepidabis harundinis umbram:
cantabit vacuus coram latrone viator.
     Prima fere vota et cunctis notissima templis
divitiae, crescant ut opes, ut maxima toto
nostra sit arca foro. sed nulla aconita bibuntur
fictilibus: tunc illa time, cum pocula sumes
gemmata et lato Setinum ardebit in auro.[18]

For Johnson in lines 21–28 gold causes a "gen'ral Massacre" (22). It brings down both the "Knowing and the Bold" (21) and corrupts and levels high and low: "hireling Judge" and "hireling Ruffian" (26, 25). In this context "Wealth heap'd on Wealth, nor Truth nor Safety buys, / The Dangers gather as the Treasures rise" (27–28) refers to the entire population, not just to the rich. When we compare to this passage the parallel lines in Juvenal, 12–14, we will be even more impressed by the width of Johnson's scope. Yes, "plures" have been undone by "nimia congesta pecunia" (12), but Juvenal has some extraordinary accumulations in mind: fortunes that are to all patrimonies what whales are to dolphins (13–14). Appropriately, where Johnson pictures gold as a "Wide-wasting Pest! that rages unconfin'd" (23), Juvenal's metaphor has it dealing out a confined and personal attack: "strangulat" (13).

In 15–18 Juvenal claims that, when the wealthy prey upon the great, the poor escape. In "temporibus diris" (15) Nero victimized rich men, including Plautius Lateranus, besieged on his estate by an "entire cohort." Juvenal ends the sentence concerning Plautius with "tota cohors," the two words beginning the line in which the topic abruptly changes to the happy plight of the poor: ". . . et egregias Lateranorum obsidet aedes / tota cohors: rarus venit in cenacula miles" (17–18). This placement makes the contrast even sharper: for the rich man hundreds of troops; a "rarus," single soldier for poor men in garrets.

Even if read without reference to the Latin satire's 15–18, Johnson's parallel 29–36 may not wholly convince us that safety lies in poverty:

> Let Hist'ry tell where rival Kings command,
> And dubious Title shakes the madded Land,
> When Statutes glean the Refuse of the Sword,
> How much more safe the Vassal than the Lord,

> Low sculks the Hind beneath the Rage of Pow'r,
> And leaves the wealthy Traytor in the *Tow'r,*
> Untouch'd his Cottage, and his Slumbers sound,
> Tho' Confiscation's Vulturs hover round.

But next to Juvenal's conviction, the mood of the imitation seems extremely tentative. First, when compared to the Latin satire's sharply defined separation of the fates of rich and poor in Juvenal's 17–18, the interrogatively phrased "How much more safe the Vassal than the Lord" becomes very much a question. One will be inclined to answer "not very" upon noting the striking divergence of "Low sculks" from "cenacula": in their garrets, where just one soldier rarely comes, the poor of the tenth satire rise *above* the "Rage of Pow'r," compared to those who lie beneath it. Finally, nothing like "Confiscation's Vulture," a metamorphosis of "widewasting pest," hovers in the skies of Rome. To the reader noting this, sound sleep for Johnson's hind does not seem a strong possibility.

In lines 37–44, based on Juvenal's 19–22, Johnson ostensibly makes the point that poor travelers need not worry about robbers on the road. Again, comparing the texts shows him considerably less confident than Juvenal:

> The needy Traveller, serene and gay,
> Walks the wild Heath, and sings his Toil away.
> Does Envy seize thee? crush th' upbraiding Joy,
> Encrease his Riches and his Peace destroy,
> Now Fears in dire Vicissitude invade,
> The rustling Brake alarms, and quiv'ring Shade,
> Nor Light nor darkness bring his Pain Relief,
> One shews the Plunder, and one hides the Thief.

First, the order differs, for the Latin passage begins with a traveler fearful because he carries a few silver dishes and closes with the empty-handed, fearless indigent who can whistle in the face of the robber (22). The imitation, however, ends with riches increased and peace destroyed. In both cases, the final impression is the stronger. Moreover, while Juvenal has two separate travelers, one rich and one poor, Johnson's envious "thee" will not allow the "needy Traveller" to be poor and happy and so curses him with wealth.

In 45–46, the first of the two couplets that close the section on gold, the plague metaphor reappears, again with nothing parallel in Juvenal: "Yet still one gen'ral Cry the Skies assails, / And Gain and

Grandeur load the tainted Gales." We are struck by the difference, because, although Juvenal makes riches the first thing men pray for, at least the prayer comes from individual fools in temples, even if in all temples (23–25). In the imitation, the prayer arises from everywhere, as if it had a power of its own and could then descend upon anyone. Even the object of Roman supplication is solid and earthborn, contrasting with "Gain and Grandeur" in the "Gales": the biggest money-chest in the forum.

After comparing these corresponding passages and entering into the dialogue with both texts that the strained applications particularly afford, one is likely to doubt that anyone in the world of Johnson's poem could evade the effects of gold merely through being poor. One is also likely to doubt that Juvenal's closing advice would have much meaning for the virtuous few who inhabit the world of *The Vanity of Human Wishes*. How can *this* life be made "tranquil" ("tranquillae") as Juvenal confidently asserts it can be in line 364, simply "per [stoic] virtutem"? One can only look toward heaven and wait. The section on gold, at least, seems compatible with the imitation's closing lines. Although one can make this interpretation without comparing Johnson and Juvenal, having compared, one has both a better reason for making it and a fuller, subtler understanding of the poem.

I intend this brief reading as a model of the way one can be led by the play of dialogue into a fuller understanding of the meaning of an imitation. This process has everything to do with the nature of the imitation, which is, in the hermeneutic sense, an "application" of the source text's meaning to the imitator's present situation. Joel Weinsheimer correctly points out that the imitation "does not merely indicate an application" of its model poem, "but is one."[19] I do not, however, agree with Weinsheimer's claim, by which he defends Hans-Georg Gadamer against Hirsch, that this proves application to be an integral part of interpretation, along with understanding and explanation. For an imitation is an answer to a question that can arise for the imitator only after interpretation of the model poem or part of it, even if only just after: how is the world of this poem like or unlike my own?[20]

But whether the imitation falls into the realm of interpretation or of what Hirsch calls "significance," it is still, as an application, the result of the imitator finding that a poem has something meaningful to say to him, because it says it to him in his world. As Weinsheimer says, when Johnson imitated Juvenal's third satire in *London*, he "validated its truth."[21] Lacking skill or will or honesty, not all imitators validated their models' truths with care. The opportunity existed, however, for poets like Johnson and Pope, and their imitations join together a mind and two worlds in a vital and fascinating relationship. In this the reader has a place and should take it.

2

Augustus

According to some scholars, Pope's time and politics so heavily conditioned his thinking on Rome's Augustan Age that modern readers wanting to understand the *Imitations of Horace* properly must reclaim his perspective. In reality, the opinions of the Augustan Age held by Pope's contemporaries were rarely so monolithically negative, even among his political associates in the opposition movement to Walpole, as many today are inclined to think. As a whole, the eighteenth-century conception was sufficiently broad and complex to allow Pope ample latitude for his poetic use and to allow him to be understood by readers who hold a variety of impressions of Augustan Rome.

In 1958 James William Johnson fired what seems to have been the first modern shot at the eighteenth-century reputation of Augustus Caesar and everything connected with him. Since then others have contributed to the destruction of the old idea that the age of Pope and Swift idolized the Rome of Augustus and Maecenas, Horace and Vergil. All of this work has been of some use, since that idea was false, but the reaction against it has been zealous, and in some cases has gone rather too far in the opposite direction.[1]

The most influential of today's revisionists is Howard D. Weinbrot, whose *Augustus Caesar in "Augustan" England* has become a book to reckon with for anyone concerned with eighteenth-century thinking about Rome's Augustan Age.[2] He has assembled an impressive collection of anti-Augustan sentiments expressed by writers and historians of the period: objections to Augustus's character and habits, to his cruelty in the early phase of his career (that is, as Octavian), and, above all, to the absolutist government he passed on to his successors. Moreover, Weinbrot shows that his court poets, Vergil and Horace, were sometimes viewed as poetically abetting their patron's despotic ambitions. No one, after reading this powerful book, would ever again call the age of Pope and Swift an Augustan Age, at least not without a pair of quizzical quotation marks like those in Weinbrot's title. However, despite the range of his evidence, his conception turns out to be as one-sided as the old, pro-Augustan, view it is intended to replace.

After 1660, Weinbrot tells us, Augustus Caesar was rarely used as an exemplar, at least not seriously. There is much praise, of course, but most of it is "balsa wood" (*AC*, p. 50), generally signifying either "vague approbation" of strong government and literary patronage (*AC*, p. 51) or a self-interested praiser—a poet angling for patronage, an administration propagandist in Walpole's time answering an opposition spokesman who attacked the king as a modern Augustus (*AC*, pp. 50, 112–13). For almost everyone the achievement of the Augustan Age as a whole became contaminated, its splendors seen as a cover-up for the hideous reality of despotism. Even Vergil and Horace came to be regarded as bad examples of corrupted talent.

And so, when Pope is writing the *Imitations of Horace* in the 1730s, both Walpole's Whigs and the opposition usually "focus on Augustus as an emblem of a bad, un-British, tyrannic ruler" (*AC*, p. 52). The opposition consistently despises Augustus, while the administration, for the reason mentioned above, sometimes wavers. Because of this attention from the politicians, the already low rating given the Augustan achievement in politics and in the arts was "gravely, perhaps fatally, undercut and often rejected" (*AC*, p. 118).

Weinbrot climaxes the chapter just cited with a set of analogies he confesses to be "extreme," but judges nonetheless "illuminating." The period considered Augustus roughly as we would consider a "Hitler [who] had won"; Vergil as we would the author of a "stunning epic . . . the purpose of which was reconciling modern Germany to the legitimacy of the new Adolphan Age"; Horace, notorious for his "alternating sexual preference," as we would a poet who had met Hitler's request for a verse epistle with a "virtuoso performance" equivalent to *Epist.* 2.1. This, of course, was the model for Pope's *Epistle to Augustus* (*AC*, pp. 118–19).[3]

I have just referred to the single most vulnerable passage in a book containing much interesting and valuable material. But its general one-sidedness needs correction and has received it from Howard Erskine-Hill's recent *The Augustan Idea in English Literature*. Although the center of Erskine-Hill's concern seems to be eighteenth-century literature, and Pope in particular, he takes a much longer view than does Weinbrot. Perhaps this perspective allows him to see that, although from the century's "middle decades on," the "diffusion . . . of the Tacitean view [of a tyrannical Augustus] was a real development," nonetheless the older and positive Augustan idea was not deeply undermined: ". . . there seems to have been no decisive move away from the older and more comprehensive sense of 'Augustan,' designating a political, social and aesthetic culture."[4]

The Augustan Idea is, of course, a great deal more than an answer to Weinbrot (and, despite appearances thus far, in this chapter I intend more than that myself). Erskine-Hill's evaluation of *Augustus Caesar in "Augustan" England* is brief, though conclusive, listing three "reservations," with which I agree.[5] Most of *The Augustan Idea,* however, opposes implicitly and in a general way the anti-Augustan position. In opposing that position here, I am going to concentrate on the period approximating Pope's lifetime and, within that span, particularly on the 1730s, the decade of the *Imitations.*

I am not interested, certainly, in reviving the old pro-Augustan extreme. My point is that eighteenth-century thinking on Augustus and his age could not have constrained Pope in any significant way. Nor did his role within the opposition to Robert Walpole constrain him; as I shall explain, the opposition was not decisively or strongly anti-Augustan. Politicians, historians, and poets all had little difficulty imagining the Augustan Age and Augustus's career as compounded of qualities and actions both good and bad.

Augustus as a Despot

Certainly few could have admired Augustus for bringing one-man rule to Rome. The age understood that he cleverly permitted the Senate and other Republican vestiges only the appearance of power; the real thing he seized for himself and passed on to his depraved successors. Given the general English distaste for absolutism, with both Whigs and Tories claiming to be the true defenders of freedom, one can expect to find no applause for the despotism of ancient Rome.

Indeed, one can infer the extent to which Augustus's despotism was deplored by sampling the opinions of several men close to Pope. Even Joseph Spence, for whom the "tranquility of [Augustus's] reign, was as a gentle dew from heaven," referred to his "usurpation." The historian Nathaniel Hooke, who also admired Augustus, criticized the "artifice [which] . . . in pretending to lay down all his power and authority got it confirmed to him." Swift, not an admirer, fiercely attacked Augustus's having "entailed the vilest Tyranny that Heaven in its Anger ever inflicted on a Corrupt and Poison'd People." Finally, in a sentence which seems capable of deterring any English citizen from trying to praise an English king by comparison with Augustus, Bolingbroke sweepingly observed that "the reigns of a Caligula, a Nero, a Domitian, an Heliogabalus . . . had never happened, if the usurpation of Augustus had never happened."[6]

Accusations most severe. What receives too little attention today, however, is a common eighteenth-century assumption about Augustus that mitigates all of them: because of protracted unrest and moral exhaustion in Rome, *an* Augustus was inevitable. Thus Spence: ". . . the temper and bent of [the Roman] constitution was such, that the reins of government must have fallen into the hands of some one person or another." To the historians, this "temper and bent" became apparent in the time of Sulla, whose career, Hooke wrote, made "those who came after him sensible that the Romans could bear a master." Swift, however, saw ominous traces of future degeneration in the Republic's earliest days, while later the Senate became "sunk in its Authority," and the people, "stirred up with the Harrangues of their orators, were now wholly bent upon Single and Despotick Slavery."[7]

Augustus Caesar was an effect, not a cause. Even Bolingbroke agreed, lamenting in his *Remarks on the History of England* that by Julius Caesar's time the Roman people had grown "ripe for slavery," having allowed "the spirit of liberty to decay, and that of faction to grow up." In the *Dissertation Upon Parties* he briefly outlined the plot, one that spanned a century. In the Republic's most prosperous days, her citizens turned to "mutual proscriptions and bloody massacres." Then, faction growing ever stronger, "the commonwealth alone grew weaker; and Pompey and Caesar finished the last tragical scene, which Marius and Sulla began." Where is Augustus in this drama? Important though he was, his place seems to be in the epilogue: after "the last tragical scene," the people merely gave him what they would have given to anyone strong enough to take it, their freedom: they "confirmed their slavery in the hands of Augustus."[8]

The emperor did not seize power from a free people: Rome was "wholly bent upon Single and Despotick Slavery" and had given up governing itself. His takeover and subsequent despotism mar his brilliance as a political and cultural leader far less than if he had staged a coup, a true usurpation, in a country truly free. In the opinion of the English, of course, England was a country truly free; at least it had issued its mandate for freedom (or reissued it, in the view of Bolingbroke and the opposition) in 1688. The differing situations helped make comparisons between Augustus and

George largely irrelevant, as shall be shown, to the issues that engaged the opposition in the 1730s.

Possibly this might not have been the case if the politicians and political journalists, looking away from the Glorious Revolution and other divergences, had managed to believe that English history was pursuing a course parallel to that of ancient Rome. A contemporary scholar has claimed, in fact, that "men like Swift, Pope, Arbuthnot, Gay, and Bolingbroke" shared a "conviction that the 'Augustan Age' of the Georges would lead to a succession of absolute, tyrannical Tiberiuses and Caligulas."[9] However, eighteenth-century minds, unlike many earlier and later, were not strongly gripped by the desire to find recurrent patterns in history. Mircea Eliade observes that, while in both the classical and earlier Christian worlds cyclic thinking about history was of great importance, "from the seventeenth century on, linearism and the progressivistic conception of history assert themselves. . . . We must wait until our own century to see . . . a certain revival of interest in the theory of cycles."[10]

Of course, no one need believe in cycles to find history instructive. In the eighteenth century, as is well known, history was studied for the sake of its instructive examples. Underlying this principle was the belief that human nature is uniform. However, since it was apparent that circumstances could vary widely, history's examples were considered instructive in a general way only. Bolingbroke, who defines history as "philosophy teaching by examples," is typical in insisting that the student of history "must rise from particular to general knowledge."[11] One did not, therefore, need a cyclic theory of history to justify comparing historical figures or events with those of the present. The *Craftsman* published several issues attacking Robert Walpole by comparing him to Pericles; readers did not have to believe they were living through an English "Periclean Age."[12]

It is no wonder that the same anti-Augustan scholar finds that the "historiographical foundation of Augustan gloom is revealed mostly in fragmentary hints."[13] We might expect greater gloom in 1660, when Charles II, in promising to take charge of his divided country, seemed more like Augustus than either George I or George II ever did, but we do not find this. In fact, Erskine-Hill shows that the poets welcoming Charles home exhibited very little interest in making comparisons between him and Augustus.[14] What mattered in history were general principles made tangible in examples. Looking at the Age of Augustus, the century saw various kinds of qualities and conduct, lessons to instruct the present, not predictions of the particular course of the future.

In trying to show that man and age were not spoiled for Pope's positive use, I have briefly discussed the period's view of Augustus as a despot. But Pope belonged to a particular political faction that, it is said, attacked George II by comparing him to the despotic Augustus. If that is so, how could Pope have used the emperor as a positive norm in his *Epistle to Augustus* or anywhere else? However, the opposition's scorn for Augustus has been considerably exaggerated, as has even its interest in him.

Augustus in Opposition Journalism

In the 1730s, when the *Imitations* were being written, Pope took an active part in opposition politics. One recent judgment that "from a political perspective, his satiric existence is an *imitatio* of Caleb D'Anvers" (fictional editor of the chief opposition journal, the *Craftsman*) undoubtedly overstates the case.[15] Certainly Pope is not always political and, when being political, he succeeds in his poetry because he is also being personal. Nonetheless, he largely shares the opposition's views and sometimes draws upon its language of innuendo, the "extensive vocabulary of disaffection minted by writers of the *Craftsman*."[16] If a strong distaste for Augustus was indeed characteristic of those belonging to the opposition, we would have grounds for suspecting that Pope was an anti-Augustan, even though we should still expect to find as a shaping force in his poetry the vision of a poet, not a politician's sense of what would play. As it happens, however, Augustus was very far from being one of the opposition's favorite villains.

The modern anti-Augustans postulate an opposition that fiercely attacked the emperor as a "violent usurper, greedy acquirer of power, and creator of subsequent tyranny" (*AC,* p. 110). This onslaught had, of course, a political purpose: to brand the king, "irresistibly" named George Augustus, a tyrant as well. Finally, it seems that comparisons between George Augustus and Augustus Caesar were frequently made: "Eagerly, the Tories scanned Roman history for evidence of the sins of the Roman Augustus in order to lay them at the door of the British one."[17]

The anti-Augustans have brought forward few examples of the two compared. A shortage of explicit comparisons is certainly understandable, since the opposition press had to guard against legal reprisals. Perhaps, then, readers understood that "Augustus" stood for "George" in the innuendo the journals regularly employed, just as they undoubtedly did understand that *"Wolsey, Menzikoff, Mackheath, Catiline, Sejanus,* et&." stood for Walpole.[18] But how many comparisons between Augustus and George were made even in this implicit way? Goldgar cites no cases and Mack only one. Even Weinbrot gives only a single example, the same one as Mack's, of a journal unmistakably meaning "George" when it says "Augustus."[19]

In fact, one finds relatively few comparisons of the king to anyone, for he was not the opposition's primary target, as Walpole, with his gallery of stand-ins, unquestionably was. Several times during his long tenure, the *Craftsman,* attempting to blame him for everything that was wrong, gave as a reason the maxim that "the King can do no wrong"; within three weeks after Walpole finally resigned in 1742, the same journal stoutly designated George "the Object of every Man's Loyalty."[20] If Walpole had not been the chief villain and—perhaps more importantly—if he had not been considered such an evil genius at manipulating George, conceivably king and emperor might have been regularly compared.

No minister led Augustus by the nose. For most of his career he directed his own affairs and Rome's; both his admirers and his detractors agreed on that. But Walpole, "the Corruptor himself" (*Common Sense* no. 273, 8 May 1742) is "the *first Mover* of the whole Machine" (*Craftsman* no. 823, 10 April 1742). As such, he easily makes a victim of the king. *"Robinarchs,"* says *Craftsman* no. 172 (18 October 1729), can overcome even a "Prince of Virtue, Fortitude, and Wisdom."

George was far from that, but even as "Jack Teazle, our *West-Country clothier,"* he is "brave and virtuous enough"; unfortunately, with "Bob Booty" (Walpole) as his "factor," "his *Enemies,* you see, *insult* him, his *Friends abuse* him, and all the World *despise* him" (*Craftsman* no. 157, 5 July 1729). Along with ridicule, he received some pity, none of which indicated that the king was blameless. In stupidly relying on an evil monster, he showed the same weakness Bolingbroke, in his *Remarks on History,* strongly attacked in previous English kings. But whether considered as pitiable victim or contemptible tool, he hardly resembled anyone's idea of Augustus Caesar.

In fact, when Augustus appears in opposition journals, which he rarely does, the quarry more often seems to be Walpole than George. In two early issues of the *Craftsman,* Walpole is probably the contemporary figure that "Augustus" represents. After qualified criticism of the emperor for his action regarding *lex majestatis,* a law against treasonable acts which he extended to words, *Crafts-man* no. 4 (16 December 1726) makes a contemporary application not to the king, but to "any Minister for the future." *Craftsman* no. 21 (17 February 1727) confronts readers with an Augustus "who grew *insolent* by Degrees, and at length *engrossed* the whole Power of the Empire into his own Hands." This sounds only partly like Augustus, who was thought to have grown steadily less insolent, and not at all like George. It does sound like Walpole, and the *Craftsman* enforces the comparison by likening this version of the emperor, whom even Weinbrot considers a "Walpolean figure" (*AC*, p. 110), to a certain *"great Man."*

Comparison could also be made between Walpole and Augustus's ministers. *Craftsman* no. 94 (20 April 1728) slyly quotes from the *Discourses* of Thomas Gordon, a Walpole supporter, on " 'mighty Caesar, to whom the *Romans* owed all their ensuing Misery and Bondage.' " Perhaps by "Caesar" the *Craftsman* intends an allusion to George, but the topic of the passage from Gordon it has chosen to print is the " 'Exaltation of [the] *Sons of Earth*,' " the conferring of great power upon their own freed slaves by all the early emperors. This may be aimed at other courtiers besides Walpole, but the *Craftsman* emphasizes elsewhere the lowness of his birth: "*Robinarchs* . . . are commonly *new Men*, of plebeian Extraction" (no. 172, 18 October 1729). The later emperors' manumitted slaves, whom the quotation from Gordon then describes—dropping Augustus entirely—resemble Walpole in both greed and power.

But although the opposition attacked the minister in what seems to be every possible way, it did not often use Augustus as one of its weapons. Since one can turn many pages of the *Craftsman* and other journals without encountering his name, he could not have been important to their writers. As propagandists charged with practical goals, they are not likely to have taken much interest in anyone in history whom they could not readily use. The logical equivalent for the emperor, after all, was the king, not the leading figure in their campaign, and he resembled Augustus in neither character nor career.[21]

Nonetheless, because of the attention the topic has received, it will not be amiss to examine what the opposition has to say about Augustus, even though he was rarely compared to George. There are a few harsh condemnations, as in *Craftsman* nos. 21 and 94, discussed above, and in 219 and 220, both written by Bolingbroke as part of the series that became his *Remarks on the History of England*. Extravagant praise of Augustus is not to be found, although Maecenas occasionally receives such praise. (For example, *Common Sense* [no. 266, 20 March 1742] once contrasted him to Jonathan Wild [Walpole] as an example of superlative worth in a minister.) On the whole, however, Augustus gets reasonably even-handed treatment.

This appears in the only, however briefly, extended comparison the *Craftsman* made between its own age and that of Augustus. The lively issue of press censorship led that journal to comment several times upon freedom of speech under Augustus, with particular reference to his application of *lex majestatis,* mentioned above, to words as well as to deeds. Although *Craftsman* no. 4 (16 December 1726) criticizes this action and claims that Augustus's bad precedent "paved the way for his next Successor to prosecute the most *innocent* Books," it points out that he himself turned the law against only "the *worst kind of Writings.*" Augustus is treated with fairness. This policy continues.

Almost two years later, responding to an attack by the *London Journal,* which cited Augustus's use of *lex majestatis* to support its case, *Craftsman* no. 117 (28 September 1728) claims that Tacitus considered this "the worst Action of that Prince's whole Reign, and the Forerunner of all that horrid Tyranny, which followed in the next." The issue refers interested readers to the "ingenious Mr. Gordon," again turning this anti-Augustan supporter of Walpole against the administration. However, balance prevails, for the *Craftsman* gives Augustus great credit for upholding freedom of speech in the early part of his reign:

> *Augustus* was at first the most remarkable Instance of any Man in History for pardoning Offences of *this Nature,* and scorning to punish any *Libels,* which were written against Him. . . . It was also a common saying with Him, *that the Spirits and Tongues of Men ought to be* free *in a free City.*

Perversion of *lex majestatis* came later, and although the *Craftsman* heaps blame upon Augustus ("the Rashness and Folly of *one Man*"), it admits that provocation was severe: "the foolish Licentiousness of one Cassius Severus (who had personally abused Him and his whole Family in a most *insolent Libel*)." It also declares, with an obvious implication, that Augustus was "influenced by wicked Counsellors."

The sequel to no. 117 is a postscript to no. 122 (2 November 1728), answering a *London Journal* riposte to the earlier issue. Again Augustus appears neither black nor white. The postscript contains a Latin quotation from Tacitus, leaving "the World to determine whether . . . it does not contain the strongest Marks of his Indignation." In fact, the quotation does not seem particularly indignant. The *Craftsman* then clears up an error in no. 117, for Tiberius, not Augustus, was "provoked" to misapplying *lex majestatis* "by the *Libels, which were published against Him and his Family.*" This denies Augustus the strong motivation which partly excused his action, but it also corrects a confusion between him and the poisonous Tiberius. Interestingly, the postscript closes by bringing Horace's *Sat.* 2.1 to the *Craftsman*'s defense, for "it appears from it that [Horace] not only attacked the *Vices,* but even the *Persons* of *wicked, great Men.*" Evidently the *Craftsman* believes that Augustus allowed his client poet to speak his mind.

Horace reappears in a purported letter to D'Anvers, in *Craftsman* no. 182 (27 December 1729), which gives Augustus almost undiluted praise. This refers to *Sat.* 2.3, in which a recent convert to Stoicism heatedly lectures the poet on the Stoic paradox that none but the sage is sane. This prompts D'Anvers's correspondent to wonder "that the *great Men* of those Times would countenance, or even tolerate *such a Sect;* the fundamental doctrines of whose Creed were a standing Libel upon the Age." However, they did, and "I look upon it as a remarkable Instance of the Lenity of the *Roman* Government, under *Augustus,* that *Horace* Himself was not taken up and called to Account for writing and publishing such a *Satire.*"

The correspondent adds that Horace must have been speaking through the Stoic, "this silly Fellow," what "He could not speak so freely *Himself.*" Presumably he thought he had something to fear. Moreover, Augustus is criticized again for perverting *lex majestatis* late in his reign, when he "abandon'd Himself to all Manner of Tyranny." Later emperors made matters worse. "Happy was it for *Horace,* that He did not live in those Days." But Horace had the happiness of living when he did, and in judging Augustus the *Craftsman* stresses not only the tolerance of that *"wise Prince,"* but the wisdom that he shared with Maecenas, for both thought *"just Satire . . .* of great Service to the Cause of Virtue; and what ought to be tolerated and encouraged under a good Government."

Given the opposition's lack of any all-embracing disdain for Augustus, or even any sustaining interest in him, no political convictions need have influenced Pope's conception of the emperor. Of course, neither opposition nor administration nor the body of citizens unattached to either side approved of his absolutism, but there is very much to Augustus besides that. The discussion in this chapter so far indicates, I believe, that Pope's contemporaries were generally able to admire what was noble in him and his age, while recognizing what was not.

This point would not seem to require much explanation. "No period," as Howard Erskine-Hill remarks, "ever thinks only one thing on a subject: it is rare for one person ever to think one thing only on a subject, even at one time." Even an average mind can see, expects to see, virtue and folly combined in the life and actions of any historical character, any real man or woman. One might believe, Erskine-Hill adds, that "in the long run the Augustan principate sowed the seeds of decline," and yet, surely, "adduce the example of Augustus and Maecenas in recommending patronage of learning and the arts."[22] One could do this without contradicting oneself and without developing selective mental blindness.

However, both Ian Watt and Jay Arnold Levine suggest that eighteenth-century minds were ambivalent or inconsistent in disliking Augustan despotism while admiring Augustan culture.[23] Howard D. Weinbrot posits a "compartmentalized response," which Pope shared with "supple" politicians; only thus can Vergil and Horace be admired, on occasion, as poets, while scorned as the tools of Augustus (*AC*, pp. 183, 141). Since the idea has achieved fairly wide currency, it merits some discussion here. The following chapter will consider the reputation of the poets, chiefly Horace. Immediately below is offered evidence that, when looking at the emperor's own character and actions, including some of his worst, the age saw a real man, not a figure painted black with unaccountable splotches of white.

Even Lord Bolingbroke, who despised Augustus, found something in him to recommend to the readers of no less a work than *The Idea of a Patriot King*. He makes Augustus one of a series of exemplary figures, including two Republican heroes, all remarkable for their "decorum." All had their vices, but each man's "was subdued and kept under by his public character." And Bolingbroke is not compartmentalizing and somehow turning away from what is bad in Augustus, for he assures his readers that by these "great examples," he intends "not to encourage vice," but to teach a virtue "essential to Princes." He can look at vice and virtue together.[24]

Nathaniel Hooke's *Roman History,* dedicated to Pope, has many good things to say about Augustus and even takes a balanced view of the young Octavian. It is true that Hooke criticizes the way in which "the *Prince* got into his hands all the jurisdiction and privileges of the several offices of the State."[25] He is appalled by

Octavian's taking the pregnant Livia from her husband, an action which "broke through all the rules of decency" (p. 320). But although Octavian's cruelty was, in fact, often complained of, Hooke insists that the "old historians" are wrong on these "particularities" (p. 294n). During the proscriptions, Octavian was reluctant to execute Cicero and may have allowed him to escape (pp. 267–68). And when Octavian beheld the bloody sword of Marc Antony, "he could not refrain from tears, when he reflected on the deplorable end of so great a man" (p. 424).

George Lyttelton, another friend of Pope's and an opponent of Walpole's, made Augustus his subject in the ninth dialogue of his *Dialogues of the Dead* (1760). Two Roman shades debate in the next world, Marcus Porcius Cato (of Utica) fiercely attacking the cruelty of Octavian and the despotism of Augustus, while Messalla Corvinus supports the princeps, as he did in life. Messalla relies on the familiar thesis that one-man rule was inevitable: after the death of Brutus, "nothing remained to my Country but the Choice of a Master. I chose the best" (p. 68).

According to Howard D. Weinbrot, "though Gibbon praised Messala [*sic*], Lyttelton used his association with Augustus to cast him into moral darkness." Cato, indeed an admired figure in the period, triumphantly "scoffs at the apparent flowering of letters" under Augustus, preferring a Rome (as Weinbrot quotes Lyttelton) under "'honest consuls, who could not read.'" At the end of the dialogue, Weinbrot continues, "Messala slinks off, finally concluding: 'I see you consider me as a deserter from the republick, and an apologist for a tyrant'" (*AC*, p. 14). However, the dialogue is more complicated than this, and Messalla does not slink off.

Messalla understands that the emperor had vices and committed crimes; he accepts much of Cato's case as true, but consistently tempers it with an awareness of Augustus's virtues: for example, "His very Ambition was *rational,* tho' it appeared to be boundless" (p. 69). Messalla's view is balanced, not ambivalent, and he firmly defends his own action in changing sides and becoming, in Cato's scornful words, the "Courtier of Octavius" (p. 67). Cato, that glorious suicide, would never have chosen a master, not even "the best," but the dialogue reveals him as unrealistic and inert, in contrast to Messalla, the practical doer of good. Cato's extreme judgment of Augustus, I believe Lyttelton wishes us to see, is not to be trusted.

"Believe me, Cato, it is better *to do some Good* than to *project a great deal*" (p. 71). This is Messalla's Swiftian criticism of Cato. Enrolled under Augustus, he himself did "some good": "[the emperor] had my Assistance. I am not ashamed to own that he had. . . . A little practicable Virtue is of more Use to Society than the most sublime Theory" (p. 71). When Cato, conceding that suicide was probably not required of Messalla, reproaches him for not going into exile, Messalla makes the same case again: "No—I did much more Good by staying at Rome. Had Augustus required of me anything base, anything servile, I would have gone into Exile. . . . But he asked no such Thing. He respected my Virtue, he respected my Dignity, he used me as well as Agrippa or Maecenas" (p. 72).

At this point Cato, who seems somewhat persuaded, volunteers the opinion that Augustus was at least better than "that Monster of Vice," Antony; for the "Egyptian Strumpet" would have ruled "if the Battle of Actium had not preserved Us from that *last of Misfortunes*" (p. 72). This is not a slight concession, for, in allowing that Augustus "preserved" Rome from the worst, Cato inclines toward Messalla's best-master argument. Again stressing his active part in saving Rome, Messalla mentions that "in that Battle [of Actium] I had a considerable Share," and that he then also helped in "encouraging the liberal Arts, which Augustus protected." Having opened this pleasing subject, Messalla challenges Cato with the grand achievement of Augustan literature: "Under [Augustus's] Patronage the Muses made Rome their Capital Seat. It would have pleased you to have known Virgil, Horace, Tibullus, Ovid, Livy, and many more" (p. 73). Here Cato counterattacks with an assertion (part of which has already been given, as quoted by Weinbrot) that I do not think most readers will find at all reasonable:

> Your Augustus and You made Rome a Greek city, another Athens under the government of Demetrius Phalareus. I would much rather have seen her under Fabricius and Curius, and her other honest consuls, who could not read. (p. 73)

Rather than something that Lyttelton might wish us to accept, Cato's words are the climactic revelation of a character marred by bad judgment and lack of effectual virtue. It is ridiculous enough to compare Augustus to Demetrius, a minor despot who managed Athens for the Maecedonian Cassander from 318 to 308 B.C. But it is totally unrealistic—it would be merely rhetorical and cynical in a less idealistic man—to long for a Rome—after all it had experienced even by Cato's time, much less Messalla's—once again primitive, pure, and illiterate. The drama of the dialogue has prepared us for this burst of passion: Cato has been giving way to Messalla; rather than allow his position to crumble further, he explodes into unreason.

Mingling respect for Cato with hinted contempt, Messalla gives him the inevitability argument again: because of "the vast extent of the Empire, the Factions of the Nobility, and the Corruption of the People . . . Cato himself, had he been upon Earth, could have done us no Good, unless he would have yielded to become *our Prince*" (p. 74). Immediately follows the dialogue's concluding sentence: "But I see you consider me a Deserter from the Republic, and an Apologist for a Tyrant. I therefore leave you to your Meditations." It is probably not fair to say that Messalla leaves Cato in "moral darkness," since he always gives him credit for earnestness. But the ending signifies not humiliation for a slinking Messalla, but a reasonable man's regret for Cato's lack of reason.

Perhaps the reader should not be entirely persuaded by the largely pro-Augustan case that Messalla presents. Although wrongheaded, Cato is a moving figure in his idealism, and he makes Messalla seem a little bit too canny. It is fair to suspect him of having chosen the princeps partly because the princeps would be a good thing for Messalla. On the whole, however, what emerges from the ninth dialogue of the *Dialogues of the Dead* is a fairly complex judgment generally favorable to Augustus and his age.

Another judgment is also implied, for Lyttelton has Cato demonstrate the weaknesses of a one-sided view. In contrast, Messalla, who seems least convincing when most enthusiastic, can recognize the blemishes in Augustus's character and career. Obviously he does not need to compartmentalize. Cato, it is interesting to note, appears unable to compartmentalize: he cannot bring himself to admire Augustan literature. The appropriate judgment on the Augustan Age, Lyttelton appears to believe, finds good and bad mixed together, as they are in most ages. This is what we see in Hooke and even in Bolingbroke. There is a similar mixture everywhere else. It seems safe to assume that the "compartmentalized response" was extremely rare.

3

Horace

What was Horace to the Age of Pope? One modern scholar has claimed that it saw a lofty sage who preached Christian morality, but this Horace is rarely to be found in the words of those who wrote about him. In general, however, at least before the advent of the anti-Augustan revisionists, he was considered to have been, if no Christian, an eighteenth-century "cultural hero" nonetheless. If the quotation marks around this phrase, appearing in one of the basic books about Pope, seem to warn against taking it literally, Reuben Arthur Brower soon puts hesitation to rest: "The Augustans saw in Horace's poetry a concentrated image of a life and a civilization to which they more or less consciously aspired."[1]

"Aspired" is too strong, and Brower probably overestimates Horace's importance in the eighteenth century, but he does not overestimate Horace's poetry. Even the conversational, unpretentious Satires and Epistles contain an abundance of insight into both public and private life. In any period, those who read these poems with care, as Pope certainly did, will indeed encounter the "concentrated image" of Rome's Augustan Age, and the following chapter will consider how Horace allows the age to appear in his work. The purpose of the present chapter, however, is to demonstrate that eighteenth-century readers did not turn to the work, as today's anti-Augustans claim they did, influenced by a prevailing judgment that Horace was an odious sycophant, servile and nerveless, especially when compared to Juvenal. Opinions varied, of course. Not everyone admired Horace, but few could have despised him, and to a good many he was indeed a hero.

Horace and the Great

Of course, Horace and other Augustan poets paid their respects to the great who patronized them, and by no means did the period wholly approve. "Let Horace blush, and Virgil too," wrote Pope, for example, informing "Heroes and Kings" that he "never flatter'd

Folks like you."[2] If the emperor had indeed been considered nothing more than a clever despot, a successful Hitler, no one could have admired his poets. We are aware, however, of the complexities within the picture of Augustus, and similar complexities occur in the period's observations on the poetic homage he was paid.

Pope, for example, also referred to Horace and Vergil in his famous letter to John Arbuthnot on satire: "Augustus and Mecoenas [sic] made Horace their companion, tho' he had been in arms on the side of Brutus; and allow me to remark it was out of the suff'ring Party too, that they favour'd and distinguish'd Virgil." This letter contains much else, including even higher praise of Augustus and Maecenas: ". . . it was under the greatest Princes and best Ministers, that moral Satyrists were most encouraged." Pope also claims that he has never thought his own "Panegyricks were Incense worthy of a Court," and he warns Arbuthnot not "to suspect me of comparing my self with Virgil and Horace."[3] As Erskine-Hill says, "Pope's words endorse no simple view of the relation of himself and Horace." It is also true, however, that "if anyone supposes that Pope looked on Horace as a flatterer and collaborator, here is clear evidence that Pope considered him a free moral satirist."[4]

In the criticism of Horace from Dryden on, one finds few charges of servility that other observations do not defuse, sometimes in the next breath. Thus, Dryden's seminal *Discourse Concerning the Original and Progress of Satire* first labels Horace "a well-mannered court-slave . . . ever decent, because he is naturally servile," then immediately muddles the verdict by offering another, offsetting, reason for him to be "decent," a shortage of material: he "had the disadvantage of the times in which he lived; they were better for the man, but worse for the satirist. . . . [in lacking] those enormous vices which were practiced under the reign of Domitian." Earlier in the *Discourse* Dryden deflects the charge of servility in advance by praising Horace's mastery of quite a different thing—the art of friendship, which made him "an agreeable companion" to the great. He praises him also, as did many others, for staying loyal in his verse to the memory of his freedman father, an assertion of low origins not symptomatic of a slavish nature.[5]

Richard Hurd refers slightingly to the Augustan "adulation of Virgil, which has given so much offence, and of Horace, who keeps pace with him." However, Hurd repeats the familiar theory that the Republic's collapse made the Roman people "ripe for servitude," and so considers the "adulation" merely the "authorized language of the times." Moreover, Horace and Vergil spoke this language "without the heightenings and privileged license of their profession." Hurd obviously admires their restraint: ". . . though in the office of *poets,* they were to comply with the popular voice . . . yet as *men,* they had too much good sense, and too scrupulous a regard to the dignity of their characters, to exaggerate and go beyond it."[6]

Praising Vergil, Lewis Crusius seems to accuse Horace:

> Surely, had Virgil intended the Aeneid as a meer Encomium of that Prince [Augustus], he might, as *Horace* has done, have made his Panegyrick at several times and of different occasions, with less expense of time and labour, than what the Aeneid cost him.[7]

But there cannot be for Crusius many examples of Horatian "meer Encomium," since earlier in his *Lives of the Roman Poets,* he praises several of the relatively few Horatian poems, all *carmina,* which may deserve that disparaging title: *Odes* 1.2, 12; 3.5; 4.5, 15. He also admires the way in which Horace expresses an evidently independent nature. Pondering the poet's motivation for *Epist.* 1.8, which obliquely warns its addressee, Celsus, to conduct himself well in dealing with a great patron, Crusius suggests that Horace "being himself above making any low advantages of his Prince's favour, and exempt from arrogance, his free spirit could not bear it in others." In reference to the "nec sermones ego mallem" passage (250–59) in *Epist.* 2.1, lines in which Horace seems to decline an invitation from Augustus to write an epic, Crusius exclaims: "See how nobly and sublimely he excuses himself to that Prince!"[8]

Dryden too admires this epistle.[9] Joseph Warton, however, finds in it not the expression of a free spirit, but "nauseous and outrageous compliments, which Horace, in a strain of abject adulation, degraded himself by paying to Augustus." He reproaches Pope, who, of course, imitated *Epist.* 2.1 in the *Epistle to Augustus,* for writing "in the advertisement to this piece [that Horace] made his court to this great prince (or rather this cold and subtle tyrant) by writing with a decent freedom toward him."[10] (It is worth noting by those interested in Pope's intentions that Warton clearly believes Pope to have meant what he said in that Advertisement.)

As a devout Augustus-hater who admired Horace and Vergil, Warton makes an interesting study. Along with Thomas Blackwell, he argues that the Augustan poets had been formed in the last years of the Republic. Surpassing Blackwell in animosity, he needlessly, obsessively, makes the same claim regarding poets who lived long before Augustus's time, including Terence (d. 159 B.C.).[11] However, this anti-Augustan extremist yet believes that close association with the court of Augustus did not destroy certain virtues in Horace that went beyond mere technical proficiency: Horace had "purity and force, both of thought and diction" and treated the "foibles of mankind with delicacy and urbanity." Warton seems to find him truly reprehensible only when he flatters.[12]

Horace had, the age understood, a fine talent for getting on with the great. His poetry lets us know that he was proud of these friends and thought he had earned them, in part, by his character. In general, the record shows that the eighteenth century agreed with him. Certainly he was amiable, "the fittest man in the world," as Spence writes, "for a court, where wit was so particularly encouraged." In the thirteenth of Lyttelton's *Dialogues* Vergil praises him: "Never had Man so genteel, so agreeable, so easy a Wit."[13] Even his politely wanton nature, his being, Crusius writes, "a little loose in his morals," could be viewed as a social asset: "His gayety, and even his debauchery," Spence concludes, "made him still more agreeable to Maecenas," whom Spence extravagantly praises.[14]

Horace's acknowledged virtues strongly offset the charge of servility: ". . . such Integrity, such Fidelity, such Generosity in your Nature," says Lyttelton's Vergil. According to Lewis Maidwell, he was a "Pattern of Filial Duty." He was by nature modest. With *Sat.* 1.6 in mind, Lady Mary Wortley Montagu commends "poor, good-natur'd, bashful *Horace*. . . . [who] never went back again, so much as to shew his Face to this great Minister [Maecenas], till he was sent for." He did not covet power and wealth, although he might have acquired them through his friends: Crusius claims that his humble station was the effect of the "moderation of his mind, not the narrowness of their bounty." Finally, he had an independent nature, the quality Crusius commends in the epistle to Celsus. "Very fond of his liberty," comments Charles Rollin, he therefore declined the position of secretary to the princeps. He also declined invitations to Rome (as in *Epist.* 1.7), even to the palace itself, as Richard Bentley remarks in the dedication to his edition of Horace.[15]

Few would disagree that Horace succeeded as a courtier partly because he succeeded as a friend, both agreeable and self-respecting, never wanting too much. His friends, of course, were the most powerful men in the world, and Pope's age generally agreed that, although Horace never held office, he did more than merely entertain them with his company and his verse. His was not an insignificant part within an alliance of poetry and power that inspired many. Gazing at the Rome that his imagination pictured, the Abbé Le Moine saw "Virgile & Horace assis à côté de ce Maître du Monde."

Le Moine was an Augustan enthusiast, but in observing that "ce Prince partageoit avec les Savans son tron, & sa puissance . . . & les regardoit comme les instruments de sa gloire," he said nothing with which those far less inspired by Augustan "gloire" would disagree, and which only someone who saw absolutely nothing good in Augustus could consider an indelible stain upon the poets.[16]

Even Joseph Warton considered the possibility that "Vergil believed it would be the best service he could . . . do his countrymen, to endeavour to soften their minds towards so mild and gentle a master as Augustus," and surely he would have made the same concession for Horace. In Lyttelton's dialogue Vergil probably speaks for the eighteenth-century majority in his praise of Horace: "You were as necessary to Maecenas as he to Augustus. . . . For you were capable, my dear Horace, of counselling Statesmen." He did counsel them, of course, and so was able "to serve your old Friends of the Republican Party, and to confirm both the Minister and the Prince in their Love of mild and moderate Measures of Government."[17]

Virtually no one, from Dryden on, really considered Horace "a well mannered court-slave." There is no reason to go on with examples. Instead, I shall turn to the question of whether Horace's satire was made to seem lacking in power and seriousness by the comparisons routinely made between him and Juvenal.

Horace and Juvenal

It is not necessary to decide which satirist was preferred at any stage in the century, if that is even possible. Did those who preferred Juvenal tend to reject Horace as a worthwhile satirist? Did Horace's reputation as a "comic" satirist who aimed at folly, compared to a "tragic" Juvenal who scourged vice, imply that Horatian satire lacked significant power or bite? Did the political opposition, favoring Juvenal, despise Horace as an "exemplar" for those within the administration "charged with answering opposition tirades" (*AC*, p. 147)? When considering Pope's use of Horace as a model, these seem to be the important questions.[18]

Some eighteenth-century critics, such as John Dennis and Joseph Addison, declined to make evaluative comparisons between Horace and Juvenal, because, as Addison wrote, these satirists were "perfect Masters in their several Ways."[19] Of the majority who did compare, many preferred Juvenal. However, rather than rejecting Horace, these usually ranked him above Persius and, in fact, just a little below their favorite. This, after all his qualifying, is finally the judgment of Dryden: with Persius in his customary position as "the last of the first three worthies," "Let Juvenal ride first in triumph . . . let Horace, who is the second, and but just the second, carry off the quivers and the arrows, as the badges of his satire, and the golden belt, and the diamond button."[20]

Admirers of Juvenal frequently make Horace "but just the second." Although in 1742 Joseph Trapp finds "the genteel Jokes of Horace . . . less affecting than the poetic Rage, and commendable Zeal of Juvenal," he believes that both, along with Persius, give "many Directions, as well as Incitements to Virtue." But while Juvenal and Horace "both agree in being pungent and cutting," Persius falters, since he "wants Poignancy and Sting." Although Crusius favors Juvenal not only because of his fiery spirit—the usual reason—but because he "is as witty and perhaps more diverting than Horace," we have seen how much this critic admires Horace.[21]

It should be remembered that Horace was usually compared to Juvenal within the context of a basically unitary tradition. Regardless of preference and despite the customary contrasts, critics usually considered the two satirists—together with less important models—not only to exemplify the resources of the genre but to share them, though in varying proportions. The Horatian and Juvenalian styles of satire were rarely considered strictly antithetical.

Therefore we should not be surprised to see Horace, despite his reputation for gentility, given credit for his power, for being, in Trapp's words, "pungent and cutting." This is not atypical praise. Horace's blade is no less keen because it is not always bared. "quem cur destringere coner, / tutus ab infestis latronibus?" (Sat. 2.1.41–42). Thus Addison: "Horace knew how to stab with address, and to give a thrust where he was least expected."[22] Although John Brown's brief history of Roman satire in his Essay on Satire Occasioned by the Death of Mr. Pope (1745) makes Juvenal the climactic figure, Brown respects Horace's artful violence:

> He cloath'd his art in study'd negligence,
> Politely sly, cajol'd the foes of sense;
> Seem'd but to sport and trifle with the dart,
> But while he sported, stab'd them to the heart.
>
> (359–62)

This is not to suggest that Horace was thought to wound coldly, without passion. In Brown's progress of satire, Horace, though "playful," nonetheless "caught the generous fire" (355) and passed it on to later satirists. In Lyttelton's fourteenth dialogue, between Pope and Boileau, just after Pope declares, "We both followed Horace," both poets agree that they were not moderate in "Panegyrick and Satire"; for "Moderation," Pope says, "is a cold *unpoetical* Virtue."[23] It is not a virtue belonging to Horace either. Walter Harte, in his *Essay on Satire,* written in praise of Pope, admires Horace, and not only because "each page instructs." For all his "courtly ease,"

> Yet Cassius felt the fury of his rage,
> (Cassius the *We[lstea]d* of a former age)
> And sad Alpinus, ignorantly read,
> Who murder'd *Memnon,* tho' for ages dead.

Juvenal, Harte then says, as he pushes on with his history of the genre, "felt a nobler rage."[24] Horace is less passionate and more instructive, more interested in correcting than flaying. But even compared to Juvenal, he did not seem weak or innocuous. This was the prevailing view, and Pope could make Horace his model without fearing that his own satire would therefore seem feeble.[25]

Regarding the two satirists, there remains the question of whether each was adopted by a rival political faction, the administration favoring Horace and the opposition Juvenal.[26] The important issue, of course, is the opinion of Horace held by the opposition. In their eyes, had Horace "indelibly become the collaborator" by "about the middle of the 1730s" (*AC,* p. 148)? Was "to be politically Horatian . . . for many opposition writers also to support an absolutist philosophy thought banished after 1688, but threatening to reestablish itself through the talents of Sir Robert [Walpole]"?[27]

Two early issues of the *Craftsman,* published a decade before Horace is held to have become indelibly stained, express criticism of him, but both are written in an apparently frolicsome mood that weakens the scorn. Although describing his *"Manners"* as *"loose and obscene,"* no. 7 (26 December 1726) also contains the surprising news that Horace was both secretary of the Roman treasury and ambassador to Gaul. This suggests an allusion to Robert Walpole, and to his brother Horatio, ambassador to Paris, but the comparison is ridiculous, since Horace never held any official position. We should not, however, expect too much from the acknowledged source of this information, a speech full of obvious mistakes made by the despised Henley the Orator, Pope's "Zany of thy Age" (*Dunciad* [B] 3.206).

No. 7 had a sequel in no. 10 (6 January 1727), consisting of a letter from a correspondent in defense of Henley, who, it seems, was misquoted on the subject of Horace's supposed offices. The earlier issue was right, however, about Horace's "Morals," which "appear to be *lewd* and *obscene*." Moreover, when the correspondent praises the poet's lack of ambition, he hints at a degraded servility: Horace "could never be guilty of so ridiculous an ambition; for he seems, through his whole works, to be fully satisfied with the Honour of being admitted into the Favour and Conversation of *Augustus* and his *chief Favourites*." On the whole, the letter deprecates Horace, but perhaps we should not take this very seriously either: it is not only a defense of Henley but purportedly the work of one "Tim Shallow."

In later issues, the *Craftsman* shows obvious admiration for Horace. No. 169 (27 September 1729) enlists him against Walpole, reminding the *"greatest Minister"* of "honest *Horace's* Rule," which proves to be *Epist.* 1.17.44–45. The lines are quoted and translated as *"There is a wide Difference between* modest Gain *and* boundless Rapine." Even Weinbrot calls nos. 122 (2 November 1728) and 182 (27 December 1729), both discussed in the preceding chapter, "warmly pro-Horatian" (*AC,* p. 149). The first salutes Horace as a brave satirist who "not only attacked the *Vices,* but even the *Persons* of *wicked, great Men.*" The second, purportedly a letter from "Phil-Horatius," designates him as Caleb D'Anvers's "old Friend." In fact, no. 182 makes Horace more than a friend: he is an exemplar for the *Craftsman.*

After Augustus, "succeeding Emperors" persecuted the authors of "all satirical Writings, whether *general* or *particular, explicit* or *implicit.* Not only *Words* . . . but even *Signs, Emblems, Hieroglyphicks, Nods, Frowns* and *Smiles* were construed, by the Imperial Advocates, into *criminal Innuendos.*" Obviously the allusion is to the administration's complaints concerning the innuendos of the *Craftsman.* Then, having established a link between the present time and the era of Tiberius and Nero, the letter considers what would have been the fate of Horace had he lived then. Like the *Craftsman,* he would have used indirect means to tell the truth; examples from the Satires are given, such as the fable of the town mouse and the country mouse and the use in *Sat.* 2.3 of Damasippus as a mouthpiece. And like the *Craftsman,* Horace would have found the truth resented:

It would have been in vain for Him to think of escaping Punishment by concealing his courtly Satire in *ironical Panegyrick:* or by dressing it up in *Allegories* and *Parallels;* or by veiling it under the Fable of a *Country Mouse* and a *City Mouse;* or putting it into the mouth of *Damasippus,* or any other *Adversary.* He would have been told, no Doubt, that *Scandal* was not the less *Scandal* for being *disguised;* that *innocent Words* were often made use of to cover *criminal Meanings,* of which his *Prosecutors were the best Judges;* and that his Writings might be *Libels,* though the matter contained in them were *true;* nay, perhaps it would have been added that They were *Libels,* BECAUSE *it was true.*

No. 182 may well be the climax, reached early in the history of both the *Craftsman* and the opposition, of a concern with Horace never particularly intense. Although Goldgar mentions one issue of the *Craftsman* (9 February 1740) in which the "essayist cites Horace as his authority for the use of ridicule on serious subjects,"[28] the opposition seems to lose whatever interest it once had in making Horace into an exemplar. However, without more evidence than anyone has yet presented, we should be wary of accounting for this nondevelopment by postulating a growing distaste for him. Where do we find, in the pages of the *Craftsman* or *Common Sense* or *Fog's,* the appropriate expressions of disgust? We will not find them in *Craftsman* no. 618 (13 May 1738), a source, hitherto overlooked, of opposition sentiment on both Juvenal and Horace. Even in the late 1730s, it seems that one could write for the opposition and yet admire both of these Latin poets, employing both as authorities.

No. 618 contains a letter to "Mr D'Anvers" from "Constans." Of its two parts, the first refers to Juvenal while likening the present to the era of Domitian, to whom George II, in an unusual instance, is clearly compared. In that evil time, knowledge of certain punishment for explicit satire compelled Juvenal to use innuendo, striking at the present by alluding to the past:

The Satirist *Juvenal* living in the Reign of a *weak, wicked* and *tyrannical Prince,* flatter'd and supported in his Vices by *profligate Ministers,* and a *corrupt Senate,* could not safely indulge his Genius in reproving his *own Age,* on Account of the numberless Swarms of *Informers,* who would soon have represented his Performance in such a Light to the *Men in Power,* as to make Him severely smart for them. In order therefore to secure Himself, and at the same Time gratify the strong Impulse of his Muse, He exposes the Vices and Follies of the *preceding Reigns,* and adapts them so well to his Purpose, that they exactly fit his *own Times,* and may be look'd upon as compleat Satires upon the extravagant Enormities of *Domitian's* Reign; though I think He mentions *that Prince* but once in all his writings.

Thus Juvenal is presented as an exemplar for the *Craftsman,* which constantly struck out at contemporaries—Walpole far more than any other—by alluding to figures from history. Constans goes on to make the ritual complaint that the administration turns every historical reference into an attack on "a *right hon. Gentleman* now living."

After some discussion, he advises D'Anvers to "humour these *captious Gentlemen"* and, instead of suggesting "odious parallels," to "draw *Comparisons* between Men distinguish'd by *military* and *civil Virtues."* Thus begins the second part of no. 618, which now proceeds toward a favorite theme of the opposition at this time, the call for war with Spain. War requires *"Steadiness in Acting,* or what we call *Resolution,"* of which several examples are given from Roman history. But before these the *Craftsman* prints a Latin quotation which "conveys [this] *Principle* universally adored tho' too seldom practiced":

> Justum et tenacem Propositi Virum,
> Non Civium Ardor prava jubentium,
> Non Vultus instantis Tyranni,
> Mente quatit solida.[29]

This is the beginning of Horace's third ode of the third book, and it displays "the perfectest Character, and most to be valued amongst the *Romans."* Clearly the *Craftsman* does not consider these lines the work of a "collaborator."

If that had been its view, Horace would not even have been quoted, but his poem is also gloriously praised according to his own standard of mixing the *utile* with the *dulce:* "This *Ode* is inexpressibly beautiful, on Account of its *Poetry;* and equally useful, for its *Doctrine.* It is admired by all Men of *Taste,* and must be so by all Men of *Integrity."* (This despite the fact that lines 11–12 describe Augustus drinking nectar with the gods.) Evidently, the fact that this number of the *Craftsman* makes Juvenal an exemplar does not mean rejecting Horace. Their names are casually linked at one point, when we are reminded that the satires of both have been used against Walpole: Constans ironically confesses to a "secret Admiration of [the] *Party-Zealots,* who can bring in . . . *Horace* and *Juvenal* as libelling the *present Minister."*

Politics are not likely to have turned Pope against Horace. Nor, despite the views of today's anti-Augustan revisionists, was the period as a whole opposed to Horace or, as we have seen, to Augustus. The modern theory is incorrect. The old conception that the eighteenth century in some way idolized the Augustan Age is also wrong, and I advocate not that, but merely the strong probability that the period's thinking on this subject was reasonably broad and balanced. Readers of Horace were therefore free, as free as readers ever are, to find and apply the meaning in his pages.

4

Reading Horace

Although Horace was often written about in the eighteenth century, we cannot be sure how often or how well he was read. Many years ago, Carolyn Goad speculated that he was less read than quoted, and quoted in small bits, such as mottoes. She considered him as "exerting his influence . . . by means of those detached utterances."[1] Perhaps Goad was right, at least for most readers; for the contemporary notion that the average eighteenth-century gentleman was steeped in Greek and Latin is largely mistaken. Given the shallowness of education in the classics, including the practice of fragmenting them for grammatical study, for many Horace may not have been a living voice at all. Even Joseph Spence had to wait until he read Pope's *Imitations* to discover that the Satires and Epistles had "a connexion and a chain of thinking in them." At school, he "had at first been used to study each of those poems in the original by piece-meal."[2]

Pope had the advantage, he told Spence, of not having gone to school, and we can be sure that he read Horace with care and understanding.[3] The *Imitations* prove that. However, most of Pope's contemporaries probably did not do a careful job of comparing these poems to the Latin source texts, and so, when modern students do this, their readings vary from common eighteenth-century readings for that reason alone. We are, however, approaching the proper goal of interpretation, the meaning Pope intended.

The following brief discussion concerns just one essential feature of the Satires and Epistles that is accessible to readers of every period and that undoubtedly meant a great deal to Pope: their treatment of the central political fact of the time, the empire itself.

The Imperial Poet

Since Pope is our concern, and since the major turn in his career as an allusive poet took him from Vergil to Horace, we will do well to consider the way in which each Augustan complements the other in regard to the empire: briefly, one expresses it large, the other small. "As Virgil is the most idealising exponent of what was of permanent and catholic significance in the time," wrote W. Y. Sellar at the end of the nineteenth century, "Horace is the most complete exponent of its actual life and movement." Compare E. K. Rand in the mid-twentieth: "In the poetry of Virgil it is rather the vision that we see; in that of Horace the fulfillment."[4]

Speaking of the imperial ideal Vergil created in the *Aeneid*, Rand adds: "If Virgil dreamed it, Horace, to whom Virgil was the half of his own soul, saw the dream fulfilled." That is, he shows his readers the Vergilian dream of empire realized on the personal level. Lewis Crusius made exactly this point regarding the two poets' "great design" of cultivating the Roman people: "*Virgil's* eloquence convinc'd them of the charms and advantages they would find in cultivating their minds and lands; and *Horace's* wit made them sensible of the happiness they would enjoy, when every man could sit and taste the comfortable fruits of his labour under his own vine."[5]

This relationship, of grand vision and individual fulfillment, seems to cast some light on Pope's assuredly complex reasons for turning from Vergil to Horace in the 1730s. Earlier, the *Pastorals* and *Windsor Forest* had clearly announced their kinship with Vergil's *Eclogues* and *Georgics* and thus the English poet's kinship with Vergil. *The Rape of the Lock* and *The Dunciad*, of course, make the *Aeneid* part of the epic backdrop beyond the mock-epic stage.[6] This use of the *Aeneid*, as a grand contrast to present-day littleness or dullness, indirectly suggests the great difference Pope saw between his own world and the imposing Augustan reality that underlies the world of Vergil's poem. Perhaps Horace's lesser version of the Augustan world, with its cultivating of minds and lands in retirement, seemed available to him at Twickenham.

At any rate, Horace is an imperial poet. It seems difficult for anyone to forget that, even when reading the *"sermones"* ("conversations"), his own rather apologetic term for the Satires and Epistles, seemingly casual poems which rarely focus directly on the grander achievements of Augustus and Rome. He even claims, in *Epist.* 2.1.250–59, that these subjects exceed his poetic powers. However, he does more than merely show the imperial dream fulfilled by expressing his own contentment and letting us assume that the empire has something to do with it. Instead, in writing about his own life, he reveals the difference the empire makes for the ordinary man—with himself masquerading as the ordinary man—by consistently taking the perspective of one who looks out upon the world from its center: "While I can, while fortune still looks upon me kindly, / I'll praise distant Samos, Chios, Rhodes— from Rome" (*Epist*. 1.11.20–21). He is always found in Rome.[7]

"Rome" is not, of course, simply a point on a map for Horace. He retains a central point of view even when contrasting his quiet rural home, which he hates to leave, with the bustling city. As the world's political center, Rome is a source of rightful order and power, expressed through those who rule the world. Although Horace's primary concern in the *sermones* is the ordinary individual's state of mind and opportunity for happiness, Rome and the empire, which allow the individual to be happy if he will, are always present. His letter to Iccius, *Epist*. 1.12, which seems typical, is brief enough to quote in full:

> As the manager of Agrippa's land in Sicily, Iccius,
> you'll gain as much there, if you take what you deserve,
> as from anything that Jove could give you. Stop complaining.
> No one is a pauper who has all the things he needs.
> If your belly's good and your lungs and feet are healthy,
> no royal treasure could add the slightest bit to yours.
> You may have turned ascetic, for all I know, and live
> on grass and nettles; you would stick to that diet
> even if you fell in Midas's stream and turned gold.
> That's so, either because money just can't affect you,
> or because you think all things inferior to virtue.
> We're amazed at Democritus, whose herds ate up his pasture
> and his fields while his disembodied soul went flying free.
> But you, although the itch for cash infects so many,
> do not think small and do care about important questions:
> What keeps the sea in bounds? What controls the seasons?
> Do the stars move in a pattern or wander where they like?
> What obscures the moon, what brings its roundness back?
> What does "concordant discord of things" mean, what do?
> Is it Empedocles that's mad or Stertinius's point of view?
> Anyway, whether you're murdering fish or leeks and onions,
> welcome Pompeius Grosphus, and if he wants something, gladly
> give it; he'll only ask for what is suitable and right.
> You can certainly afford to be friendly to a decent man.
> Now I'll fill you in on Rome's affairs and get you current:
> The Spaniards have yielded to Agrippa, the Armenians
> to Tiberius, equally strong. Phraates, on his knees,
> has accepted Caesar's rule and law. On Italy
> Golden Plenty pours from laden horn abundant fruit.

Iccius, in Sicily, has been complaining, about what we cannot be sure. "Stop complaining," Horace tells him and adds, in a tone best described as locker-room-Epicurean, that if his belly, lungs, and feet are in good shape, he should be happy enough. Horace comments on Iccius's philosophical studies, which are made to seem slightly grandiose. The request that Iccius welcome Pompeius Grosphus is another way of exhorting him: get out of yourself; let us have no more complaints and, unless it begins to affect your actions, no more philosophizing. The epistle might have ended here. Horace has given advice to a friend who appears to need it, but since Iccius lives far from Rome, this letter ends by giving him, in its last five lines, the latest news.

This coda, placing the empire briefly in the foreground, demonstrates why complaints are out of order. It does so by echoing the theme of Anchises' great speech on Rome's role in book six of the *Aeneid:* Rome's mission is to bring order to the world, to pacify and rule the nations and peoples, including its own.[8] Even nature seems to realize this, rewarding Italy from "laden horn." The Roman peace allows Iccius to grumble safely in Sicily. It would also allow him to achieve contentment; only we can give ourselves that, as Horace often says, but an orderly world provides the opportunity. As Horace tells Bullatius, a traveler, in the eleventh epistle: "What you seek is here, / it's at Ulubrae [a small Italian village], if you maintain a balance in your soul" (29–30). If he chooses, Iccius can cultivate this balance in the soul, this "animus . . . aequus."

As Horace does. In *Sat.* 2.6, which Pope and Swift imitated together, he describes his peaceful life in the country, comparing it to a day in Rome. In just a few lines, as the poem begins, he makes his rural happiness felt:

> I prayed for this: a measure of land, not very big,
> with a garden and, by the house, a spring whose waters
> never cease, and a wood just above. Greater than this
> the gods have wrought, and better. Good. I ask for nothing more.

At this point Augustus and Maecenas, the empire, may seem far away. However, as the *sermo* proceeds, it subtly establishes a firm connection between the greater Roman order and Horace's simple life.

The empire enters *Sat.* 2.6 in the sketch of the day in Rome (20–58), where everyone Horace meets is aware of his powerful friends. One rude character, whom he accidentally jostles in the street, even taunts him: " 'Go ahead, knock everybody down! / Getting back to Maecenas is all you think about' " (30–31). In Rome all wrongly believe that he has inside information, for which they pump him, and that he knows if the Dacians will invade (53), knows even the plans of Augustus: "'What about the vets? Will the farms that Caesar promised / be in Sicily, or will he offer them Italian land?'" (55–56). Thus Horace reminds us of Augustus as Rome's defender (who else would defend against invasion?); as the victor in the civil wars (the veterans are his); as a patron of agriculture and a settled life, turning his soldiers into farmers, after years of violent confusion.

Through the references to Augustus, *Sat.* 2.6 gives us glimpses of Vergilian Rome, the empire large. In the picture of his own life in the country, Horace gives us the human side, the promise of empire fulfilled. He lives well there, partly because he is wise enough to "ask for nothing more," but also because the empire provides him and everyone else with stability, following a century of trouble, and with enlightened leadership. It has provided Horace, in fact, with his beloved farm, through the gift of Maecenas, who has an important place in this poem.

Since Horace is known to be particularly close to Maecenas, the unenlightened assume that the poet can use his influence with the minister to do them favors (38–39). Of course they misunderstand. As Horace explains in an aside to his readers, whom, as usual, he ranks above most of humanity, his friendship with Maecenas excludes considerations of this sort:

> The seventh year, more like the eighth, has now flown past
> since first Maecenas added me to the circle of his friends,
> to keep him company in the carriage when he traveled
> and be his confidant for these remarks: "What time is it?"
> "You think the Thracian Bantam [a gladiator] can give Syrus a good fight?"
> "If you don't dress warmly, this morning air can really bite."
> These are safe state secrets for a leaky ear like mine.
>
> (40–46)

Horace soon reveals that his neighbors in the country accept him with the same easy intimacy. Unlike the city people, who always seem to have an angle, they are direct with him and with each other. (The contrast is summed up in the fable of the city and country mice that ends this *sermo*.) At dinner on Horace's farm, all are "released / from silly rules" (68–69), released, one can see, not just from rules that govern drinking (the immediate context), but from any restrictions on the honest exchange of thoughts and feelings. Souls are cultivated through the discussion of such questions as "'What brings men happiness, virtue or much wealth?'" (73).

Perhaps Horace implies criticism of Maecenas, along with the self-deprecation of "leaky ear," for seeming to prefer trivia to homely but serious topics of this kind; in *Epist.* 1.1 he openly reproves the great minister for a related failing—paying too much attention to appearances. If criticism is Horace's intention here, it shows, as it does there, concern for a friend. But whether or not Horace is criticizing, he makes it plain that he can simply be himself with Maecenas just as much as with his humble neighbors in the country. Equally at home with both, in *Sat.* 2.6 he himself connects the great Roman world with the lesser world of rural Italy and his own "measure of land, not very big." His "Bene est" ("Good") in line 4 refers to both orders of existence, great and small, both actually parts of a single thing.

I will not say that every satire and epistle makes us think of the empire, but most do, if only by mentioning one of its great men. As a body, the *sermones* illustrate what centralized and benevolent power can mean to the individual. Augustan power is for Horace, obviously, an example of power rightly used. Readers are likely to take it in that way too; they certainly will if they want to understand what Horace meant to say and show in these poems. For that power has much to do with the Horatian life, one of the most influential examples of the good life in all literature.

Examples, as E. D. Hirsch, Jr. has recently reminded us, enable literary works to speak to the future and thus make application possible for readers in the future. Examples are concrete, of course; they are particular cases. But they are also members of a class or concept, and this may have different exemplifications in the future. Therefore,

> the true extension of a literary intention is not restricted to its original exemplary element. That would be a contradiction in the principle of exemplification itself and would make impossible genuine future readings or genuine future fulfillments of the original textual intention.[9]

Hirsch endorses Philip Sidney's conception of the poet as a teacher who combines general precepts with examples.[10] This is certainly an apt description of Horace, whose *sermones* instruct us, as he intended, because we understand both his precepts and his examples. The latter are necessarily oriented toward the future, for Horace had the future well-being of his readers in mind when he wrote about himself and Rome. Presumably he had in mind human happiness in general, and that is not bounded by time. He is his own greatest example of human happiness, and Horace's greatest achievement is to make this exemplary self, for all its rootedness in a particular time and place, stretch out forever, forever alive.

Now, while presenting himself as an example, he also presents and recommends the kind of political power that supports him—one of an indefinite number of examples, all belonging to the general concept "political power." Strongly centralized and extremely effective, benevolent, absolute Augustan power unites poets and political leaders, placing both at the very top and center of the state: Augustus and Maecenas, Horace and Vergil.

Reading Horace in the *Imitations of Horace*

Pope saw this exemplary power in the Satires and Epistles because it is there to be seen. Horace obviously intended no allusion to its degeneration under the later emperors, and the *Imitations* will tell us if this historical fact mattered to Pope as he read the *sermones,* his models. I do not believe it did. The *sermones* do indicate that Augustan power is absolute, a literary (and historical) fact that undoubtedly limited its appeal for Horace's imitator, but there is no reason why Pope should have objected to its being centralized and strong. Detecting the presence of Augustan power, realizing what it means to Horace, we will be better prepared to understand Pope's vision of another kind of political power, that which prevailed in the age of Walpole and George.

The contrast between the two is severe and is an important part of every one of the *Imitations.* First, balanced against Horace's Augustan power, the power of the English court is made to reveal itself as a potent source of disorder. Second, the contrast explains why we are so strongly impressed by the doubleness often remarked on in the *Imitations,* as Pope opposes his own high ideals to the unappetizing realities he perceives in both society at large and the court: to this doubleness, we contrast the model *sermones'* relative singleness. Although Horace is critical of the blind strivings of most men, he appears confident that those in power share his ideals and will be guided by them in their public policy. In contrast, the English court leads the country ever farther from any approximation of the ideal in practice.[11] Finally, Pope's apparently gradual recognition of his own moral isolation, compared to Horace's quite different situation, creates much of the complexity and interest of the *Imitations.*

This last point may require some discussion before it is illustrated by referring to the *Imitations* themselves. For reasons the following chapter will briefly review, Pope began this series of satires intending to assert a similarity between Horace and himself. To a degree, which diminishes as they proceed, he keeps to this purpose, before finally dismissing Horace as a model in the *Epilogue to the Satires*. He begins, then, with a substantial measure of Horace's confidence that others will listen to him as he articulates his beliefs. But even at the beginning, as I will demonstrate, he cannot find in the world any significant signs of the order and sanity that he finds in his own private life at Twickenham. The contrast with Horace's case helps us to realize this and its importance.

Horace finds no essential distinction between the world and his home, between riding with Maecenas and dining at the Sabine farm with neighbors. Where Horace is, Rome is. He is a moral poet, and his world has a high place in it for moral poets. Although most people, like the Roman crowds in *Sat.* 2.6, will not listen to him, a significant minority always will, and this includes the Augustan court. Since Pope's situation vastly differs, none of his attempts to assert a similarity between Horace and himself ever quite succeeds. What we get instead, in all of the poems, is something much better, a relationship more complex and interesting than any honorific identity could possibly be.

As we read the *Imitations,* we get a sense of Pope's growing concern, of "an increasing strain in the poet's voice."[12] This is much more than the symptom of an imitator's frustration at failing to present an accurate Horatian image. What upsets Pope is the knowledge, of which he seems to gain more with every imitation, that he matters very little in a world where power lies apart from him; this lesson acquires its point from the contrast with Horace, that other moral poet, in *his* world. Fredric V. Bogel admirably expresses what the contrast means to Pope as a man:

> Pope takes Horatian assumptions as an image or background against which he depicts his own struggle to achieve what Horace assumes or can achieve with greater ease: an ordered self, or the ability to endure disorder; an acceptance of the depredations of time; an understanding that the man of vision is always alienated, and therefore that vision and experience always require to be wed anew.[13]

Horace more easily achieves or simply assumes these things because he sees greater order in the world around him and understands how intimately he is connected with its source. His "assumptions" lead Pope to test his own.

In the first imitation Pope likens himself to Horace in a world that, he sees, will allow the comparison to be no more than partial. He can try to live at Twickenham as Horace did on his Sabine farm, but since the greater orders, Rome and England, vastly differ, Pope's domestic situation really differs from Horace's. Rome supports Horace, who, even when living alone in the country, remains part of its ruling circle. But the court of George, and with it, by extension, the nation it misrules, opposes Pope by disregarding or threatening everything he values. Therefore, even at the beginning, the rural peace he pictures seems less than substantial, his Horatian pose of contented self-acceptance something of an illusion. It becomes an increasingly desperate one.

As a satirist, Pope is profoundly affected by having to confront Horace's truth of a sustaining power that allows good men and good poets to stand within the center of things. With each imitation he makes manifest the consequences for him and the world of there being no such sustaining power where he is, and the poems show him altering his sense of his duty and his proper methods in satire to conform to this reality. Eventually the *Imitations of Horace* show him confounded by it, unable to function at all. No wonder we sense an "increasing strain" in his voice.

I do not, of course, pretend that Pope was surprised by what he wrought in the *Imitations,* as if learning for the first time with each one that his situation was a little less like Horace's than he had previously thought. Even in the first of the series, he goes out of his way, through strained applications, to point out important differences between Horace and himself. However, the *Imitations* themselves, as the concrete results of juxtaposing the two worlds, in all probability helped to darken his view of his own. There is a great difference between the cheerful aggressiveness with which the *Imitations* begin and the mixture of anger and resignation that fills the *Epilogue to the Satires.* Pope had other reasons for increased gloom, surely, but five years is not a very long time, and neither his fortunes nor his friends' sank so quickly as the mood of his Horatian poems.

The *Imitations* reveal Pope constantly attempting to adjust his satire to the kind of power operative in his age, while retaining some resemblance to Horace in his style and persona. Horace's contrasting methods and presence in the model poems bring out the desperation and, in some instances, the incoherence of Pope's efforts, which end with the implicit admission that no satire can achieve anything: nothing can penetrate the thick heads and hard hearts of those who would hurry the world into darkness.

*   *   *

Joseph Warton wrote that in the *Imitations,* Pope "resembles in his style, as he did in his natural temper, the severe and serious Juvenal, more than the smiling and sportive Horace."[14] Scholars today who may differ on other matters concerning the *Imitations* concur in finding "Persian and Juvenalian conventions" in "poetry that can combine Horatian and Juvenalian, and something like Persius."[15] The present interpretation of these poems will, however, contain few references to Persius or Juvenal.

But it is possible to exaggerate the importance of these satirists to the reader of the *Imitations.* No one, of course, would conclude that, whenever Pope seems angrier or sterner than Horace at a particular point, he therefore has become like Juvenal or Persius. His employing a "convention" that Persius or Juvenal also used is not proof of allusion either. It seems to me that, if Pope intended Juvenal, for example, to come to the forefront somewhere in an imitation, to be a presence equal to Horace, then the reader should be able to locate a specific reference to one of Juvenal's satires. But this we can rarely do. We cannot do it without study in any case, since the Latin text is not before our eyes, so that Samuel Johnson's objection to the disadvantage of the *Imitations* for "common readers" applies much more clearly here.[16]

Finally, while Pope may indeed allude to anyone he wishes, the *Imitations* show him "basing himself in the Horatian original," as Erskine-Hill points out.[17] Horace was fundamental for Pope and is also fundamental for the reader who compares the two texts. The dialogue one overhears between imitation and *sermo* becomes most interesting when Pope and Horace sharply differ; these differences matter more for the reader, who then significantly enters the dialogue, than a resemblance, often rather vague, in tone or style between Pope and someone else. The following chapters will concentrate on the "strained applications" that reveal and in part account for Pope's growing conviction that his satire cannot even hurt his enemies, much less improve them, and that the darkness gathering over his country will envelop Twickenham too.

5

Beginning

The First Satire of the Second Book of Horace
Imitated

By the early 1730s Pope was a satirist, whether he had wanted to be
one or not, and faced with the eternal need of the satirist to
convince others that he is righteous, or at least right, not cranky,
misanthropic, or mad. When the *Epistle to Burlington* roused feeling against Pope for libeling the Duke of Chandos, his host at
Cannons, as Timon, he wrote and published an *Imitation of
Horace,* the first of the series. Bolingbroke had remarked to Pope
"how well [Horace's *Sat.* 2.1] would hit my case if I were to imitate
it in English," and Pope took his advice.[1] But this was not the first
Horatian satire to which Pope had turned for a satirist's self-de-
fense. His "Horace, Satyr 4. Lib. 1. Paraphrased," which made
twelve English lines out of *Sat.* 1.4.81–85, appeared in the *London
Evening Post* in January 1732. Later inserted with some changes
into the *Epistle to Dr. Arbuthnot* as lines 289–304, this describes a
false friend who "sees at C–n–ons what was never there."[2]

The fourth satire of Horace's first book seems in some ways
remarkably appropriate for Pope. First, it gave him Fannius, the
self-promoting poet who, as Lord Fanny, represents Lord Hervey in
the imitation of 2.1, where one finds no Fannius. (Pope mentioned
later that 1.4 was his source [Butt, p. 4].) Second, in this satire
Horace's complaints concerning Lucilius's careless haste in composition (7–13) might have been an opportunity to bring in Dryden,
who, Pope would later write, "wanted, or forgot, / The Last and
greatest Art, the Art to blot."[3] Perhaps the opportunity to make
Dryden his Lucilius did not attract Pope, since he makes little out
of a similar opportunity in *Sat.* 2.1. But he surely was attracted by
Horace's splendid tribute to his "pater optimus" (105–26), who
resembles Pope's father, also humble, also virtuous, as he appears
in the *Epistle To Dr. Arbuthnot.*

Why did Pope not imitate the entire *Sat.* 1.4? The question may

seem too speculative, but the satirist's defense unused may suggest
something about what Pope saw in the one he chose. The striking
difference between 1.4 and 2.1 lies in the contrasting status each
apology for satire accords the genre. In 1.4, when first responding
to the charge that, as a satirist, he enjoys inflicting pain (34–37),
Horace seems neither to confront the charge nor even to evade it
adequately. He simply denies that the satire he writes ought to be
considered poetry:

> In the first place, I don't count myself among those
> I consider poets; it's a mistake to think that putting words
> in meter is the only thing they do, or that anyone
> like me—my things are more like conversations—is a poet.
>
> (39–42)

The poem develops this theme through line 63. Although a digres-
sion, it is a most conspicuous one, and when Horace returns to the
charge of sadism, which he then answers rather well, he does not
do so by exalting either the genre or himself.[4] In need of what
"would hit my case," Pope chose an apology that does exalt, or
seems to. In *Sat.* 2.1, satire becomes a weapon wielded by a hero:
"Qui me commorit (melius non tangere clamo) / Flebit, & insignis
tota cantabitur urbe" (45–46)[5] ("[Anyone] who gives me any trouble (my motto is 'Hands off!') / will become a tearful celebrity, sung
about all over town"). At least, Horace postures heroically. But his
words are so uncharacteristic that modern scholars question his
seriousness. "Behind the pugilist's gloves," writes Niall Rudd, "we
can detect a mischievous grin." Edward P. Morris, in his edition of
the Satires and Epistles, errs in considering the whole poem an act
("there is not an argument that is meant to be taken seriously"), but
he seems to me right in detecting the message behind the show of
pugnacity: "the satire becomes . . . a kind of proclamation by
Horace of his assurance that his writings need no serious de-
fence."[6]

Pope valued Horace. The third chapter above supplies proof that
he meant exactly what he said in the Advertisement to the *Imitations* in his collected works: "An Answer from *Horace* was both
more full, and of more Dignity, than any I cou'd have made in my
own person." *Sat.* 1.4, however, may have lacked the "Dignity" he
sought, while the manly stance of 2.1 is somewhat suspect. We
cannot tell how seriously he took Horace's show of toughness and
valor in this satire, but that the poem is unusual in making this show
is something he must have realized. Searching for his "Answer from

Horace," perhaps Pope sensed, even at the beginning of his rather brief span as an imitator of Horace, that modeling himself after the Augustan satirist would not be simple.

Most of *The First Satire of the Second Book of Horace Imitated* follows its source, but in a complicated way. Numerous gaps occur because Pope grounds his poem in his own time and place far more than did the average imitator or, for that matter, Horace himself. Thus he has more proper names than Horace; for example, there are three in "P.'s" opening speech, while in the equivalent lines Horace has just the indefinite "quibus" and "altera . . . pars." However, the reader can fill most of these gaps so that parallels result: between Rome and England and, as Pope intended, between Horace and himself. Several modern critics have made thorough comparisons that show how Pope usually establishes likeness.[7]

Rather than attempt further interpretation along these lines, this discussion will focus on two difficult, unsettling cases of unlikeness that belong in the class of Samuel Johnson's "strained applications": Pope's omitting of a true contemporary equivalent for Lucilius, Horace's exemplar and alter ego, and his ascribing of great importance, based on nothing parallel in the Latin satire, to his own home. Despite the similarities between source and imitation, these gaps suggest fundamental differences between the roles and, perhaps, the destinies of Pope and Horace.

Lucilius first appears, in line 17, as an example given by Trebatius, the partner in the dialogue, who briefly urges Horace to praise Augustus's peacetime achievements—as Lucilius did for Scipio Africanus. Since Lucilius is not of major importance here, Pope's omission of an equivalent for him in Fortescue's corresponding lines (29–31) seems not important either. Lucilius becomes significant, however, in the Latin 24–34. After Trebatius asks why Horace writes satiric verse that makes all fear and hate him (23), the poet claims that satire is simply the particular enthusiasm, out of a vast number of human "studia," that captivates him:

> Quid faciam? Saltat Milonius, ut semel icto
> Accessit fervor capiti numerusque lucernis.
>   Castor gaudet equis; *ovo prognatus eodem*
> Pugnis: quot capitum vivunt, totidem studiorum
> Millia: me pedibus delectat claudere verba . . .
>
> (24–28)

> (What can I do? Milonius dances when he's drunk, the heat increasing in his boiled brains, the lamps before his eyes.

Castor's joy is horses, his identical egg-mate loves boxing;
of the thousand things that men like doing, each man
finds his own. My pleasure is arranging things in meter . . .)

Like the long evasion in *Sat.* 1.4, these lines obviously run the
risk of making satire appear trivial; the risk seems deliberately
taken since Horace compares his own enthusiasm—which, in addition, is made to seem merely mechanical as in the earlier satire, a
"metering"—to passions for drink, boxing, and racing. However,
this apologia takes a different course when Lucilius reenters the
poem, as he immediately does. Horace arranges his "things in
meter,"

Lucili ritu, nostrum melioris utroque.
Ille, velut fidis arcana sodalibus olim
Credebat libris; neque si male gesserat, usquam
Decurrens alio, neque si bene: quo fit ut omnis
Votiva pateat veluti descripta tabella
Vita senis. Sequor hunc, Lucanus an Appulus anceps.

(29–34)

(in the style of Lucilius, a better man than you or I.
Long ago he made his books his faithful friends and to them
trusted his most private thoughts. In good fortune and bad,
he never rushed to other confidants. So, in his work we see,
as if upon a votive tablet, the old man's entire life.
Him I follow, unsure if I'm Lucanian or Apulian.)

Here there is no "mischievous grin" behind the gloves. Line 29
refers to the father of Roman satire in unmistakably reverential
terms. The first meaning of "ritus," of course, is "religious custom"
or "ritual," and the "nostrum melioris utroque" refers not to rank,
since Trebatius (if not Horace) held high rank, nor to poetic skill,
but to character. The rest of the passage establishes Lucilius as a
writer committed to the honest revelation of his own being. Willing
to set his own failings down along with his strengths, he therefore
qualifies morally for the task of criticizing others. The impulse to
write satire, which the puzzled reader has seen described as a kind
of bad habit, becomes understandable as a product of profound
honesty.

Now, truly successful satire requires more than that. By the
comparison to a votive tablet, a painting, usually crude, giving
thanks to the gods for deliverance from danger, Horace probably
meant to suggest the point he explicitly makes in *Sat.* 1.4 and 1.10,

that Lucilius lacked poetic skill.[8] But the stress here falls not on his failings, but on his greatest virtue. The "old man" is better than either of us because of the simple wholeness of his vision. Therefore Horace says "Sequor hunc" and means it. He then flies off into a discussion of his own origins, as if embarrassed by having compared himself to so pure a soul. His meaning is clear, however: Lucilius is his exemplar in satire, and the essence of satire is revealing the truth.

I have commented on these eleven lines of Horace in some detail to show the importance of Lucilius there and to help make clear how much Pope has varied from his model in his own 45–62. For he has no Lucilius figure, and he plainly becomes his own exemplar. Possibly, because of other changes, he may not need a Lucilius simply to dignify his satire: he refers to no mechanical metering, and lines 45–50, rather than merely associating satire with various "studia," concentrate on attacking the individuals who exemplify these. However, his straining of the application is nonetheless apparent after line 50. Although in 59–62 Pope promises to save his work on "Vice too high" for publication after his death, that threat hardly compromises his pledge to expose *himself,* Lucilius-like, now:

> I love to pour out all myself, as plain
> As downright *Shippen,* or as old *Montagne.*
> In them, as certain to be lov'd as seen,
> The Soul stood forth, nor kept a Thought within;
> In me what Spots (for Spots I have) appear,
> Will prove at least the Medium must be clear.
> In this impartial Glass, my Muse intends
> Fair to expose myself, my Foes, my Friends.

> (51–58)

While Lucilius is Horace's exemplar, the comparisons with Shippen and Montaigne seem almost incidental. There is no "nostrum melioris utroque" for them, no "Sequor hunc."

Some interpreters have treated this gap as insignificant, while others try to make Shippen and Montaigne reasonable Lucilius-equivalents. The discussion above of 2.1.29–34 suggests that Lucilius means too much to Horace for the first interpretation to be very probable. The second requires speculating rather freely about what Montaigne and Shippen may have meant to Pope.[9] It is apparent, however, that in this imitation he says much less about them than Horace does about Lucilius, and that his perspective on them is not reverential in the manner of "Lucili ritu."

G. K. Hunter and Howard Weinbrot recognize this gap between source and imitation and consider it fairly important. One may question, however, the ways in which they account for it. Weinbrot argues that Pope gives himself no predecessor because "Horace's Lucilius praises a major figure in the government."[10] But since the government in question was that of the Republic, this thesis should not impress even the most fervent anti-Augustan. Hunter asserts that Pope "could easily have found a modern parallel [for Lucilius] in Dryden," but, seeking to present himself as a "Romantic" individualist, the poet "chooses not to appear as the follower of another satirist."[11] There is, however, a more plausible explanation. When Pope does mention Dryden (113–16), he stresses, as I shall explain, the dependency inherent in being the laureate; this kept Dryden from uttering the whole truth.

Dryden might have been a likely candidate for the office of Pope's Lucilius if something besides candor had been central to Horace's portrait of his predecessor in satire or, evidently, to Pope's portrait of himself. That being the case, however, Pope could hardly say "Sequor hunc" of Dryden. Perhaps he did not wholly choose to create this gap. He did not create Dryden's laureateship. Perhaps constraint was as important as choice: in the process of imitating he looked for an equivalent he could not find. If so, Pope may have altered, subtly to be sure, his own sense of how he fit into his world: by looking for but finding no Lucilius, he engages the fact of his own rootlessness as a moral satirist, compared to the ancestry Horace proudly claims in Lucilius.

Of course Pope is proud too, as the reader doubtless perceives. Contrasted to Horace, who stands behind Lucilius, he stands *out* before us as a solitary figure, alone in English tradition; solitary, he is therefore both more heroic than Horace and more vulnerable. Noting this, we are likely now to feel some uncertainty about the meaning of the entire imitation, in which the comparison between Pope and Horace is fundamental. This uncertainty will probably increase when we recognize that in his 105–33 Pope again provides no equivalent for Lucilius, again central for Horace in the lines imitated, 62–74.

When Trebatius warns Horace that writing satire may get him into trouble (60–62), he responds with uncharacteristic fire—and with Lucilius:

> Quid? cum est Lucilius ausus
> Primus in hunc operis componere carmina morem,

Detrahere & pellem, nitidus qua quisque per ora
Cederet, *introrsum turpis.*

(62–65)

(What! When Lucilius, first
to compose poems of this kind, dared to strip the skins
from those who dazzled all the men they walked among,
though filthy underneath.)

Horace goes on to say that Lucilius would inflict this punishment on all who deserved it, even "*Primores* populi" (69) ("the people's leaders"), because he was "UNI AEQUUS VIRTUTI ATQUAE EJUS AMICIS" (70) ("he favored virtue only and virtue's friends"). Virtue's friends included, however, some of the most powerful men of the time; Laelius and Scipio are named here as approving of the satire (65–68) and befriending its author (71–74). Lucilius did not risk a great deal.

One easily grasps the implication that Horace too has an attachment to virtue, and that he has his own great supporters and friends. This would be clear even if he did not make the connection explicit in line 74, when "ego" finally makes an appearance. Until then, however, it is Lucilius that stands before the reader. In contrast, although Pope's version of the passage begins with the literal "What?" for "Quid?," as if to prepare for an uneventful imitation, "ego" promptly appears in the very same line: "What? arm'd for *Virtue* when I point the Pen" (105). It never withdraws. "To VIRTUE ONLY and HER FRIENDS, A FRIEND" (121) is said of Pope. He briefly mentions Boileau and Dryden, but, as client poets, they hardly resemble Lucilius, no client, although his friends supported him, and Pope does not imply that he himself is like the modern poets. In fact, he is much better, because he is free:

> Could pension'd *Boileau* lash in honest Strain
> Flatt'rers and Bigots ev'n in *Louis'* reign?
> Could Laureate *Dryden* Pimp and Fry'r engage,
> Yet neither *Charles* nor *James* be in a Rage?
> And I not strip the Gilding off a Knave,
> Un-plac'd, un-pension'd, no Man's Heir, or Slave?
>
> (111–16)

This is a declaration of moral, as opposed to political, strength: no one owns him, unlike those he names. I admit one can think of another poet who had a monarch to write for; Pope is suggesting, how purposefully we cannot be sure, that he is more at liberty to tell the truth than was Horace, if not Lucilius. Moreover, although Lucilius was no client, since he and his friends had political power, Pope, who lacks it, may seem braver than he. Thus, for a moment Pope implies that he is both different from and better than either Roman satirist. Something similar occurs at two other points in this passage.

In 62–65, quoted above, Horace says that Lucilius stripped away, not the masks, but the "skins" of wicked men to show the filth *"introrsum"*: not behind, but literally "within." The language characterizes him as a bloody-handed, violent satirist, and we know that Horace is too amiable and too artistic (he has reminded us that Lucilius lacks art) to carry on for very long in just that way. Although in his line 115 Pope does appropriate some Lucilian violence, for he "strip[s] the Gilding off a Knave," in rendering Horace's 62–65 he makes his own satire seem like neither Lucilius's nor Horace's; instead, he is lofty:

> What? arm'd for *Virtue* when I point the Pen,
> Brand the bold Front of shameless, guilty Men,
> Dash the proud Gamester in his gilded Car,
> Bare the mean Heart that lurks beneath a Star.
>
> (105–8)

There is no abstract "virtus" in the Latin being imitated, and the verbs Pope uses—"Brand," "Dash," "Bare"—sound positively noble compared to *"Detrahere & pellem"* ("to strip the skins"). When rendering Horace's picture of Lucilius at ease with the great (71–74), he elevates again. Scipio and Laelius enjoyed "nugari cum illo, & discinti ludere" (73) ("joking and playing with [Lucilius]").[12] Horace does not want us to understand that he, a freedman's son and client poet, has sported in Lucilius's way with Maecenas and Augustus. They are his friends, not his equals. "Cum *magnis vixisse*" (76) ("lived among the great") avoids specifics. Pope's more detailed treatment does present his friends as his equals, or perhaps as slightly less than that; however, the behavior of host and guests is more formal than the "joking and playing" of Lucilius and his circle: Pope and Bolingbroke share, along with "my friendly Bowl," both the "Feast of Reason and the Flow of Soul" (127–28). There is something stately in Peterborough, as he "Now, forms my Quincunx, and now ranks my Vines" (130).

Pope differs in his style of satire from both Horace and Lucilius, modulating away from both in the direction of formality. One might say he is being like Juvenal or Persius in this respect and, in addition, that his style in recreation resembles what we might consider congenial to them.[13] However, *Sat.* 2.1 does not give Pope much chance to establish himself as a modern Juvenal or Persius or anyone else *against* Lucilius and Horace. These two satirists share with each other an allegiance to good and an aversion to bad that he obviously wishes to claim for himself. There is no room for Pope to oppose them in the all-important matter of virtue.

The important contrast with them concerns his safety. Again, simply by having no Lucilius figure, Pope makes himself singly visible and therefore vulnerable. He also becomes more heroic, of course, and is not loath to seem so. When he renders Horace's praise of Lucilius for attacking important men, he gives substance to and makes more formidable the highly generalized "*Primores* populi": the "Gamester in his "gilded Car," the "mean Heart" concealed by a "Star," the "Knave" whose "Gilding" he will "strip" (107–8, 115). He makes the conflict between satirist and target seem more personal than it is in 2.1, which accordingly lacks an equivalent for Pope's vow that "while I live, no rich or noble knave / Shall walk the World, in credit, to his grave" (119–20). His powerful enemies are his country's enemies too. He is right to attack them, but since he lacks what both Lucilius and Horace had—an alliance with virtuous power, one wonders if he can do it with impunity.

When Horace tells Trebatius that Laelius and Scipio approved of Lucilius's satire (65–68), one has no difficulty recalling who Horace's own powerful friends are. At this stage, the imitation contains a gap, for the parallel lines 109–14 make no reference to anyone who seems likely to support Pope. First Pope calls upon distant leaders in whose existence, considering the allegiance between power and vice he has just attacked in 105–8, we cannot easily believe: "Can there be wanting to defend Her [Virtue's] Cause, / Lights of the Church, or Guardians of the Laws?" (109–10). Compared to the source, this sounds vague and hollow. Then, in making the implicit contrast between himself and the clients Boileau and Dryden, Pope mentions Louis, Charles, and James (111–15), but he obviously foresees no support from George.

Pope's friends do appear when, following Horace, the imitation turns to the subject of relaxation in a "Retreat" (125), Twickenham. Peterborough and Bolingbroke, those good men, exemplify the categories of "Chiefs, out of War, and Statesmen, out of Place" (126). The modifying phrases beginning with "out" show Pope deliberately straining the application, creating a gap that is not, however, difficult to fill: in his time, which differs in this respect from two eras of ancient Rome, power does not go to those morally qualified to use it. Pope attacks those who have it, is befriended by those who should. But without it, how can they protect him, as Horace and Lucilius were protected? This question brings us to the related theme of the two opposing orders of England and Twickenham.

As noted, "ego" finally makes an appearance in the Latin line 74. Reinforcing the point implicitly present in the preceding lines on Lucilius, Horace states that, since he too associates with those who hold and are morally qualified to hold high power (the highest power, in this case), sharp-toothed Envy cannot hurt him:

> —Quicquid sum ego, quamvis
> Infra Lucili censum, ingeniumque, tamen me
> Cum *magnis vixisse* invita fatebitur usque
> Invidia, & fragili quaerans illidere dentem,
> *Offendet solido;*—
>
> (74–78)

> (Whatever I am, no matter how
> inferior to Lucilius in talent and in rank, I too
> have lived among the great as envy must admit;
> seeking a soft morsel to sink her teeth into, she'll bite
> on something hard in me)

We have been impressed with Pope's exposed, solitary position, compared to Horace's. However, although the English passage begins with Envy, the poet seems not to fear her, for he gives her no teeth and no real life:

> *Envy* must own, I live among the Great,
> No Pimp of Pleasure, and no Spy of State,
> With Eyes that pry not, Tongue that ne'er repeats,
> Fond to spread Friendships, but to cover Heats.
>
> (133–36)

Envy has lost her power to hurt, Pope explains: "And who unknown defame me, let them be / Scriblers or Peers, alike are *Mob* to me" (139–40).

Yet the imitation began with his complaints about attacks on him which Envy helps to generate: envy in the talentless (like Fanny/ Hervey) of the talented, in the bad of the good. So did Horace begin, but by his lines 74–78 we fully understand how little harm "Invidia" can do him: his friends are good men who happen also to be supremely powerful. Pope cannot say this, of course, since his "Great" are out of power. As a satirist, he might have armed himself against Envy with the sharp teeth he took from her; but, in a complex echo of Horace's lines, he claims to have, instead of teeth, the eyes and tongue of one who presides over beloved subjects. Although Horace does not so much as mention his own home, Pope presents himself as the benevolent ruler of a little kingdom, a lesser order, that offers dignified refuge from the world and the envy in it to both the "Great" and himself.

This is entirely characteristic of Pope, for whom Twickenham is a potent symbol of virtuous retirement. Dustin H. Griffin refers to it as "a counterkingdom," opposing Walpole's England, and G. F. C. Plowden, in discussing two of the *Imitations,* has characterized the poet as "the *opifex rerum* of his own world."[14] Nonetheless, no matter what Pope does in his own territory, outside of it Envy should still have teeth. His enemies, if he has really hurt them, will not respect the rank he gives himself. We must wonder how long the world will let Pope vex it. This question obviously concerns Pope too and is part of what prompts his initial request to Fortescue: "You'll give me, like a Friend both sage and free, / Advice" (9–10).

Fortescue, however, is not much help. Although plain-spoken at the imitation's beginning, at its end this "Council learned in the Law" (8) greatly outdoes Trebatius in confusing legalese (145–48). Finally, he leaves matters up to Pope, as if he were, not a "Friend," but a fellow lawyer: "See *Libels, Satires*—here you have it—read" (149). This after warning him first that the law's letter may not help: for "Laws are explain'd by Men" (144). In this poem Pope has to provide his own answers, and these seem hardly conclusive.

How long will the world let Pope vex it? We are not given a simple answer. Possibly for a long time, if it changes for the better, and it might, since Twickenham represents a possibility of national rejuvenation. First, the very presence of Peterborough and Bolingbroke, England's proven leaders, offers some hope. Each is considerably past his prime (Peterborough was seventy-five years old when this imitation appeared); but by preserving the statesman and the general, Pope's Twickenham preserves their ideals and keeps their influence alive. Pope himself, however, is obviously the most important person present, as proprietor and refuge-giver, and as a satirist. For although he does not picture himself writing satire at Twickenham, obviously the place preserves him in some way and lets him carry on with this virtuous work.

Whether Pope's satire can change the world outside, the greater order, depends on his audience, who probably do not overlap with his satiric targets. The latter are the unworthy, gilded great, and the poem holds out little possibility that Pope can actually shame anyone in this class into mending. He speaks here of stripping, of revealing; the question is, who will notice? Here we see some minor, but interesting differences from Horace. While *Sat.* 2.1 has Lucilius stripping off the lying skins "per ora" (64), "before men's faces," the imitation omits any direct reference to an edified audience for Pope's satire. However, Pope also omits any equivalent to "*populumque* tributim" (69) ("the people, tribe by tribe"), whom Lucilius attacked along with the "*Primores* populi." In this satire, Pope does not deny the possibility that virtue may inhere in a "populus" whose eyes his satire may open and whom Bolingbroke may some day lead.

But suppose Pope and Twickenham have no significant effect? How long will his enemies, all the powerful scoundrels his satire unmasks, leave him and it alone? While Peter Walter, Francis Chartres, and Lord Hervey seem only to arouse Pope's contempt at the beginning of his poem, the alliance of vice and power they represent impresses him further on, as we have seen. His final reply to Fortescue addresses the question of his own survival, but it cannot possibly mean what it seems to mean:

> *Libels* and *Satires!* lawless Things indeed!
> But grave *Epistles,* bringing Vice to light,
> Such as a *King* might read, a *Bishop* write,
> Such as Sir *Robert* would approve—"
>
> (150–53)

This suggestion of powerful connections satisfies Fortescue, who chooses to forget what he must know, since so many know it: whoever the bishop is, the king is no reader, and the minister is not likely to approve of satire that supports the opposition. But we should not be satisfied—with this answer, that is. For the poem's uncertainties, which seem to me to show Pope's real, not assumed, lack of certain knowledge concerning his effectiveness and his fate, contribute to its drama and give it much of its life.[15]

We might further consider his relationship with George, who will not support Pope, but from whom any action against him seems unlikely. Although Pope facetiously claims to write satires that a "*King* might read," this king will not. No verse, we are assured in this imitation, can interest George or his family. After linking his military exploits with the sorry rhymes of "rumbling" Blackmore and "wild" Budgell (23, 28), Pope sums up the interest in poetry which grips the "Royal Line" (32):

> Alas! few Verses touch their nicer Ear;
> They scarce can bear their *Laureate* twice a Year:
> And justly Caesar scorns the Poet's Lays,
> It is to *History* he trusts for Praise.
>
> (33–36)

We perceive a certain fitness. If a good poet toiled for George and the royal family, his lays would be scorned too, but the laureate is Cibber, who deserves to be despised. At least Pope has a good chance of being left alone. No one in the court wants any Hanoverian epics or royal birthday odes from him, or from any other poet, and Fortescue's brief suggestions (21–22, 29–32) that he write such things lack seriousness. (How could Pope be expected to "lull with *Amelia's* liquid Name the Nine"?) The king, unconcerned with poetry, may well let him write whatever he pleases.

Comparison with Augustus, however, will quickly make this possibility seem less encouraging. In *Sat.* 2.1 Horace first claims he lacks the talent to write heroic verse about Augustus's martial triumphs (12–15), then tells Trebatius he will approach the emperor with poetic praise of his peacetime achievements only if the poem is good; Augustus will resent anything that is not (17–20). Evidently, Horace can decline to write poems that praise him; the poet, the client poet, has his freedom, more than one can assume Cibber does or Dryden did. This is one accurate measure of Augustus's worth as a patron and as a ruler. Another is the fact that his achievements both on the field and on the domestic front are worth writing about (10–11, 16). Finally, he takes a genuine interest in poetry and can judge it.

Because of the contrast, George's lack of interest seems positively unnatural in a king: his indifference to poetry and to the figure he makes in poetry suggests indifference to achievement in all of his affairs. Dullness is immanent in him, and dullness in the king, dullness in the state's very center, may pose a threat to everyone—even the poet-king of Twickenham. In the *Epistle to Dr. Arbuthnot,* Pope shows himself besieged by the scribbling masses. These dunces pursue their passion, as other dunces other passions, other kinds of "studia," because no responsible central authority directs their actions.

In *The First Satire of the Second Book of Horace Imitated,*

Twickenham seems safe from dunces. In fact, when Pope describes his tranquil life at home, he seems to forget who misrules the country, just as he also apparently forgets the enemies he has made by his satire. Still, he may have been disturbed, as his readers may be, by a basic opposition between the world of Horace's *Sat.* 2.1 and his own world, with its two opposed orders. In Horace's Augustan Age, we see just one all-embracing order: the Sabine farm does not need to become a separate center. Poetry and power obviously intersect in the age, not only in Augustus, but in the client poet, Horace. Since Horace is a satirist, satire and power intersect; we know who Horace's friends are. And we know who Pope's are and where they are—at Twickenham, not the court. Rome's Augustan stability is opposed to a divided society, with the wrong party holding the power, that thus appears impermanent by comparison.

Pope undoubtedly thought of himself as both a skillful satirist and a virtuous man, and he thought similarly of Horace. He did not, of course, begin to compose this imitation in the belief that he was anything like an eighteenth-century English incarnation of the Roman poet. There is simply too much difference between their situations relative to everyone and everything around them. By forcing the comparison with Horace, however, through the act of imitating, Pope raised questions concerning the effectiveness of his satire and, more vaguely, of his chances to live and write as he liked.

Extremes: Ofellus and the Rake

The Second Satire of the Second Book of Horace Paraphrased

After the imitation of *Sat*. 2.1 appeared, Pope expressed contempt for it in letters, calling it an "idle poem" and a "slight thing." Perhaps these unmerited slurs were intended to turn the attention of his correspondents toward the *Epistle to Bathurst,* on which, he wrote in several of the same letters, his labor was long and hard.[1] However, they may also signal discomfort with implications that, as I have tried to show, possibly arose for him in applying *Sat*. 2.1 to his own world and his role there.

That *sermo,* moreover, presents an uncharacteristically pugnacious Horace, not quite the serene imperial poet visible in most of the other *sermones.* Possibly Pope was reluctant to make a clear contrast between this Horace and himself, and thus raise the issue of how serene he himself could be in his age and circumstances, for he chose as the model for the second of the *Imitations,* written in 1734, another atypical satire. *Sat*. 2.2 is the only *sermo* in which Horace employs a spokesman or *prolocutor.*[2] This is Ofellus, a countryman who farms as a tenant the land he used to own.

For most readers, however, Ofellus does not become an individual, distinct from Horace, until line 94 of Pope's Latin text.[3] Until that point both the tone and the principal subject, the Roman fascination with exotic food, often reveal sophistication inappropriate for a simple farmer. This, the greater, portion of *Sat*. 2.2, "while it conveys some impression of [Ofellus's] homely speech . . . makes no effort to create a consistent illusion."[4] Afterward, however, Horace chooses to let the farmer speak in what seem to be his own words and out of his own experience. Lines 94–96 are a stage direction ending with "Videas, *metato* in agello" ("See him on the little farm they took away"). Ofellus then begins: "Non ego, narrantem, temere edi luce profesta / Quidquam praeter *olus,* fumosae cum pede pernae" (97–98) ("'I never used to eat,' he says, 'on an average working day / anything but some cabbage and the end of a smoked ham' "). Until the poem's end, at line 116, he speaks for himself.

I shall have little to add to the existing analyses of the imitation's rendering, in 1–128, of the Latin lines 1–93. As John Aden has pointed out, this part of the English poem contains political satire.[5] However, the satire is not notably specific, and Pope has used less detail here than elsewhere in the *Imitations;* one sign of this is an unusually low ratio, for him, of 128 English lines to 93 in his abridged version of the Horatian text. This part of the poem deserves the *"Paraphrased"* of the title. In contrast, the concluding 52 lines render just 22 in his source and paint, first, a rich, if fanciful, picture of Pope's life at Twickenham, then a nightmarish vision of a national decline that includes politics but goes beyond them. Lines 129–80 constitute the full-fledged imitation that will be my study here. It poses Pope and Pope's world against Horace (through Ofellus) and the Augustan Age.

One difference between the two conclusions is easy to detect. Where Ofellus speaks for himself, Pope appropriates the speaking part, displacing his Ofellus, Hugh Bethel. We become sure of this upon reading line 137: "Content with little, *I* can piddle here" (emphasis added). However, this development should not surprise us greatly, not so much as the similar displacement of Lucilius in the first imitation, since Pope prepares for it. While Horace in his 1–93, though obviously altering what Ofellus might have said, does not talk about himself as the alterer, in the equivalent lines Pope occasionally reminds us that a poet is at work. He presents himself, in a parenthesis, making plain speech into something finer: "Now hear what blessings Temperance can bring: / (Thus said our Friend, and what he said I sing)" (67–68). He reports that the "Friend" praises simple dining because "ev'ry Muse" will come to the poet next morning, and also allows "just indulgence" for one "tir'd in search of Truth, or search of Rhyme" (84, 86–87).

Moreover, Pope resembled Horace's Ofellus in living on land belonging to another, while Bethel owned his own land. Interpreters of this imitation, well aware that Pope has taken over Ofellus's part, consider the poet's status as renter a satisfactory explanation for the change.[6] This may well be so. But no one has tried to account for the additional gaps that can be observed between the Latin 94–116 and the English 129–80. These considerably strain the application, revealing great differences not only between the self-described rustic lives of Pope and Ofellus, but also between their perspectives on the intertwined fates of land and men. The effect is to strengthen certain doubts, first apparent in the imitation of *Sat.* 2.1, concerning Twickenham's capacity to serve both as a haven for Pope and for others and as a center for national renewal.

Of course there is also a strong likeness between the situations of Pope and of Ofellus. Both lead simple lives. In 97–105 the farmer describes his diet and dining customs:

> Non ego, narrantem, temere edi luce profesta
> Quidquam praeter *olus*, fumosae cum pede pernae.
> At mihi seu *longum post tempus* venerat hospes,
> Sive *operum vacuo*, &c.—bene erit, non *piscibus* urbe petitis,
> Sed *pullo* atque *haedo*; tum—
> > —*pensilis uva* secundas
> Et *nux* ornabit mensas, cum *duplice ficu.*
> Posthac ludus erat Cuppa potare Magistra,
> Ac *venerata Ceres*, ut culmo surgeret alto,
> Explicuit vino contractae seria frontis.

(In his Latin text Pope has omitted several words; my translation will bracket the omissions.)

> ("I never used to eat," he says, "on an average working day
> anything but some cabbage and the end of a smoked ham.
> But if after a long absence a friend would come to visit
> or [a welcome neighbor,] on [rainy] days when we couldn't work,
> we used to eat well, not on fish shipped from the city
> but on chicken and kid. The dessert tables had raisins
> and nuts to dress them up, and some split figs too.
> Last came a drinking game with each man his own master
> and a toast for Ceres—'Rise high on towering stalk'—
> as she unknit with wine the wrinkles on our brows.")

Here Ofellus recalls the old days, when he owned land, but the point of his whole speech is that, although the farm is now another's property, he carries on in the same way. Since his life was simple then, "Quantum hinc imminuet?" (107) ("How can [Fortune] diminish that?"). And Pope too, although "My lands are sold, my Father's house is gone" (155), claims to be happy and self-sufficient at Twickenham.

But Ofellus is a working farmer, and his work controls his life. He describes his meager diet on an "average working day"; he eats more substantial fare with farmer neighbors (more often, one would think, than with long-absent friends) when rain prevents work. Hard labor put those wrinkles on their brows; they enjoy their ease just as, if all are like Ofellus, they gladly accept the work. At

Twickenham, however, no one works or needs to, for lines 141–50
present a place where food appears at the poet's command and
dinner seems, not a break from toil, but a magical test of diners'
souls:

> 'Tis true no Turbots dignify my boards,
> But gudgeons, flounders, what my Thames affords.
> To Hounslow-heath I point, and Bansted-down,
> Thence comes your mutton, and these chicks my own:
> From yon old wallnut-tree a show'r shall fall;
> And grapes, long-lingring on my only wall,
> And figs, from standard and Espalier join:
> The dev'l is in you if you cannot dine.
> Then chearful healths (your Mistress shall have place)
> And, what's more rare, a Poet shall say *Grace*.
>
> (141–50)

No farmer, Pope establishes a relationship with nature by showing
her bearing for him at his command or of her free will. Walnuts,
grapes, and figs harvest themselves, and for other food he need
only point. Under his roof dinner becomes a ritual singling out the
impure, who "cannot dine"; presumably, Pope's *"Grace"* protects
the dwellers in Twickenham from the forces the "Poet," as satirist
rather than mage, assails in the imitation's first two-thirds.

The willingness of edibles to be eaten shows the influence of the
Ovidian story of the Golden Age. We understand and accept the
convention. There are signs, however, that Pope wished to deem-
phasize the distinction concerning work. He omitted from the Latin
the reference to rain, which controls the working farmer's activities;
also omitted is a scene-setting line (115 in the conventional text, 97
in Pope's, had it been included): "cum pecore et gnatis fortem
mercede colonum" ("his animals and sons there with him, a tough
old hired hand"). This description not only stresses Ofellus's hard-
iness, but, by grouping men and animals together, indicates how
perfectly integrated Ofellus is within nature. But flocks are tended.
Ofellus finds his being in nature through work.

Mindful of literary convention and of the powers that traditionally cling to poets and rulers, we may grant Pope his mana, but
the presence of Ofellus, even in an edited text, will probably keep
us from having much faith in it. For Pope's protective and nurturing
powers seem insubstantial when compared to the solid truth we
recognize in the farmer's life and labor. The vatic power threatens to
become poetic haze and dissipate against the granite of Ofellus,
who works and endures through work, not by casting a spell upon

his land. Pope's claims of self-sufficiency and security do not seem insincere, but they do seem somewhat desperate and unconvincing. This perception is as available to Pope, comparing the two texts, as to any other reader.[7]

Perhaps affected by this consideration, rather than offering a "portrait of his deep inner contentment" on his land, as one critic would have it, Pope claims less for this enchanted Twickenham than he does for the "Retreat" pictured in the first imitation.[8] There, while Bolingbroke and Peterborough are displaced, these honored guests still represent the classes "Chiefs" and "Statesmen." The unnamed visitors in the imitation of *Sat.* 2.2 are, in contrast, weary refugees on whom the poet takes pity: "But ancient friends, (tho' poor, or out of play) / That touch my Bell, I cannot turn away" (139–40). In such as these there seems no potential for England's renewal.

By straining an application, Pope seems further to emphasize the ineffectuality of these visitors to Twickenham. It is no surprise, of course, that in 156–64 they take the place of Ofellus's sons, since Pope had no sons. (In 163 he allows Swift, briefly summoned into the poem as a friendly *adversarius,* to sympathize with one who had "'to build, without a son or wife.'") At first, the passage conveys the idea present in the source. "quanto aut *ego* parcius, aut *vos,* / O pueri nituistis, ut huc *novus Incola* venit?" (107–8) ("'how have I suffered, or you, / my sons, in health and spirit, since the new owner came?'") becomes:

> My lands are sold, my Father's house is gone;
> I'll hire another's, is not that my own,
> And yours my friends?
>
> (155–57)

The reader will then note, however, that while the "pueri," extensions of Ofellus, live and work on the farm, Pope immediately stresses his guests' transiency:

> thro' whose free-opening gate
> None comes too early, none departs too late;
> (For I, who hold sage Homer's rule the best,
> Welcome the coming, speed the going guest.)
>
> (157–60)

Sat. 2.2 has nothing like this. Howard Erskine-Hill believes that Pope makes his gate open freely, both ways, to strengthen Twickenham's positive associations: the Horatian theme of retirement joins with the English "country house ideal," which incorporates the motif of frequent comings and goings.[9] But there is so much stability in the situation of Ofellus and his sons, permanently wedded to the land, that the guests seem, by comparison, unsettled, rootless, weak.

Why has Pope chosen to strain the application? Possibly because he wishes to suggest that these virtuous friends, however weary, are badly needed in the corrupt world outside. Although the suggestion would be stronger if he had boldly asserted here, as in the first imitation, that they had been deprived of their rightful positions, the reference to "sage Homer's rule" supports it. Since, as Butt notes (p. 67), the rule Pope has in mind is given by Menelaus in his kingdom of Sparta to the visiting Telemachus, the imitation associates the greater order beyond Twickenham with unruled, chaotic Ithaca. But although Telemachus, led by Odysseus and favored by Athena, found success in Ithaca, we cannot confidently predict the same for "ancient friends, (tho' poor, or out of play)"; they have no warrior kings or goddesses on their side.

They have Pope, of course, a poet-king with certain pretentions to divinity, but the contrast with the farmer has already led us to suspect his strength; moreover, the concluding and climactic fourteen lines of the imitation show an England even more resistant to reform than Ithaca. So depraved is this greater order, in fact, that the continued existence of the lesser, of Twickenham as a safe refuge, seems threatened. For in 167–80 Pope turns into the most despairing satire a passage which, in the Latin, is far removed from that.

In the last eight lines of the Horatian poem Ofellus distills from his life's experience a philosophy of acceptance that easily rises above the issue of whether he or Umbrenus, the "illum" of 109 below, owns the farm. It is based on the conviction that man and land will always endure:

> Nam *propriae telluris* herum natura neque illum
> Nec me, aut quemquam statuit; nos expulit ille,
> Illum aut *Nequities,* aut *vafri inscitia juris,*
> Postremo expellit certe *vivacior* haeres,
> Nunc ager *Umbreni sub nomine,* nuper *Ofelli*
> Dictus, erit nulli proprius, sed cedet in usum
> Nunc mihi, nunc alii. Quocirca vivite fortes!
> Fortiaque adversis opponite pectora rebus.
>
> (109–16)

("The land has no owners: nature never granted him a title, she gave no rights to me or anyone. He pushed us out;

his sloth, or his ignorance of our complicated law,
a surviving heir, if nothing else, will push him out.
Now this land is named after Umbrenus; Ofellus was
the old name. It belongs to no one, but lets itself be used
now by me, now by others. So then, live, live and endure.
Meet life's difficulties with strong, enduring hearts.")

To point out that Ofellus recognizes no difference between *dominium* and *ususfructus* hardly describes the firmness of his faith. Men and years will always expel one owner and set up another, but Ofellus's long view shares the perspective of nature herself. The land will always be there and will always let itself be used by someone. Land and men of the land endure, and Ofellus now speaks as one of the latter, transcending—as literary examples must—his own time and place.

In contrast, Pope shows both man and land in precipitous decline. "What's *Property?*," he asks, and answers, "dear Swift! you see it alter / From you to me, from me to Peter Walter" (167–68). When the moneylender Peter Walter becomes the final owner, the land does indeed "alter," becoming mere *"Property,"* just another item in a list of assets. In most of the metamorphoses of ownership that Pope presents, the land alters in this way:

> Or, in a mortgage, prove a Lawyer's share,
> Or, in a jointure, vanish from the Heir,
> Or in pure Equity (the Case not clear)
> The Chanc'ry takes your rents for twenty year:
> At best, it falls to some ungracious Son
> Who cries, my father's damn'd, and all's my own.
> Shades, that to Bacon could retreat afford,
> Become the portion of a booby Lord;
> And Hemsley once proud Buckingham's delight,
> Slides to a Scriv'ner or a City Knight.
>
> (169–78)

And in every case, it seems, title passes to worthless owners, blind to the traditional, vital link between man and land. The "best" outcome is succession by a son who damns his father, indicating disrespect for all tradition. After Bacon, eventually, comes a "booby Lord," and after Buckingham, Hemsley "Slides to a Scriv'ner or a City Knight," alien to the land. Ownership continues, but use, which Pope celebrates elsewhere, most clearly in the *Epistle to Burlington,* seems to stop. As a result perhaps, in an odd echo of the magic within Twickenham, the land outside of it seems mysteriously to change its character. It becomes a "Law-yer's share" or a consideration in a "Case"; it can even fall out of existence altogether: ". . . vanish from the Heir [or air?]." Since all of this unwinds next to the Latin poem's vision of land eternally yielding to use by the race of Ofellus, the contrast makes land in England seem literally denatured, fatally altered by man's blindness to what it really is.

This concluding passage does not seem to me to contain specifi-cally political implications.[10] In any case, the satire extends beyond politics, and those affected by the decline Pope envisions extend beyond the class of landowners. The lines indeed "sketch a dark future for men . . . who lived on their inherited estates," but they are not the only inhabitants of this future.[11] It is all of England that "slides." In widening his focus, Pope has not allowed his own noninherited land to remain visible, so that we are less prompted to wonder how it can preserve the mythic inviolability already made problematic by the contrast with the willing labor that sustains Ofellus and his farm. But how could it resist an apparently universal fall? Possibly the final couplet is meant to imply that Pope will lose Twickenham: "Let Lands and Houses have what Lords they will, / Let Us be fix'd, and our own Masters still."

At any rate, these lines are too pessimistic to be "a proud declaration of mastery,"[12] a description that a comparison with Horace's conclusion makes still more unlikely. Ofellus, of course, could not imagine the separation of land from worthy users (and its consequent transformation into *"Property"*). Land is eternal for him, and he is part of the land. Thus he can counsel strength and endurance as his *sermo* ends: "Quocirca vivite fortes! / Fortiaque adversis opponite pectora rebus" ("So then, live, live and endure. / Meet life's difficulties with strong, enduring hearts"). This is a credo of cheerful resistance to obstacles that, if they cannot be overcome, cannot overcome us. In contrast, Pope appears to counsel a glacial stoicism. He does not counsel resistance, and so appears to lose faith in the force of the satire that occupies much of his poem.

In discussing lines 129–80 I have contrasted Pope to Ofellus, who speaks in the equivalent Latin lines. It is understood, however, that Ofellus speaks for Horace, who shares his philosophy and lives on his own land in a way that the farmer's life somehow reflects. But when one looks for Horace behind Ofellus, one sees a poet who is not so intimately connected with his land, although much of his work reveals a closeness with nature, as he is part of the larger political order of the Augustan Age. (So, in fact, is Ofellus, for he contributes to the stability that even his humble existence requires.) Horace has, of course, a close connection with the great, while Pope is at odds with those who dominate in his age.

Given this truth, rather obscured because the contrast with Horace is not direct, one has good reason for doubting both the power of satire to oppose the destructive forces beyond Pope's gate and the ability of Twickenham to protect the poet from them.

Sober Advice from Horace

From the sturdy virtue of Ofellus, Pope then moves to a much racier set of standards in the model for *Sober Advice from Horace* (1734), *Sat*. 1.2. Like the Horatian satires Pope had previously imitated, this too would allow him to avoid confronting the fully Augustan Horace, the established satirist who speaks for power. In this early *sermo* Horace does not yet speak as a court poet with a home in the country, since he has yet to enter the court or be given the home. Moreover, the poem is mildly obscene and was therefore considered disreputable—not the work of the best Horace, or possibly of the "real" Horace.

Of course one could argue that *Sober Advice* is not the work of the real Pope. The voice that addresses us in this imitation seems less like that of the Pope we hear in other poems than that of a rakish persona, perhaps, as G. Douglas Atkins has suggested, a rake with a "strong attraction to the Restoration," to which the poem often alludes. The fact that Pope continually denied authorship suggests that he wanted to put some distance between himself and the speaker of *Sober Advice*. However, it is probably a mistake to think, as Atkins does, that this persona is "the butt of much of the poem's satire."[13]

First, the speaker never takes the center of the stage, as Ofellus eventually does. We see the world he describes, not him living in it. Second, although Atkins believes that the speaker "unwittingly dramatizes" his own inner disorder through his caricatures of women, actually Con. Philips, Jenny, and the others are typical of the creations Pope conjures up in angry or even simply playful moods.[14] Finally, while Pope at his gravest would disapprove of much of what the speaker says, Pope is often very far from grave, and the speaker has, for that matter, some spasms of morality. Rather than an embodiment of qualities Pope entirely dislikes, this persona is more likely to represent an aspect of his creator. At any rate, he seems alarmed, as the Pope (or Popes) we know in other texts would be alarmed, by what the poem reveals: the weakened state of both human reason and traditional moral standards.

Despite the view of the majority of critics, *Sober Advice* is serious satire. This becomes clear when we juxtapose source and imitation to bring out the critical differences between them. At its beginning, Pope's poem gives us monsters in the place of Horace's merely human fools. It then proceeds to assert that society has no firm standards governing sexuality, while *Sat.* 1.2 assumes the opposite case. Finally, Pope accounts for the monsters and the lack of standards by suggesting that humanity is not in close contact with nature, which Horace characterizes as accessible to anyone who chooses to live and think rightly.

Horace's lines 1–30 present a gallery of foolish and miserable males who exemplify extremes in behavior: one is a spendthrift, another a miser, one a sloven, another a dandy, and so on. The extremists of Pope's equivalent 1–38 are primarily female, but this sexual difference is less important than that between the normal human folly of the Horatian gallery and the grave deformity rooted in the souls of Pope's rather terrifying collection.

Pope indicates moral perversion through physical description, employing images far more bizarre than anything in the Latin passage, vivid though it is. Where the Roman epicure (7–11) sacrifices all he owns to a demanding "ingrata . . . ingluvie" (8) ("ungrateful gut"), the synechdochic organ of Con. Philips functions with the frightening directness of a dream: "And Lands and Tenements go down her Throat" (14). "*Rufa's* at either end a Common-Shoar" (29) is a strangely distorted echo of Horace's pair of fools who wear their tunics respectively too low and too high (25–26). *Sat.* 1.2 has no one equivalent to "bashful *Jenny*," who "ev'n at Morning-Prayer, / Spreads her Fore-Buttocks to the Navel bare" (33–34). "Fore-Buttocks" alone might be "gloriously comic,"[15] but by having her spread them and then pointing to the navel to confuse Jenny's anatomy further, Pope makes her image, admittedly an assault on the female form, stand for the utmost distortion within.

This distortion, which all share, also reveals itself through their actions. Pope's characters tend to do more harm, to others and to themselves, than do their counterparts in the *sermo*. Horace begins with the deceased Tigellius, lamented by the mob, who was too generous for his own good. Mourned by "all the Court in Tears, and half the Town" (3), Anne Oldfield must have also suffered from some species of generosity, probably sexual. However, she "Could joyn the Arts, to ruin, and to please" (6), while Horace says nothing of Tigellius's ruining anyone. The opposite extreme to prodigal Tigellius, stingy "hic" (4), will not help a needy friend, but at least he has not made him needy, unlike his equivalent. More aggressive, she "of Ten Thousand gull'd her Knight" (7), not once, but twice; then she wasted it all (which "hic" would never do) on a "Gallant" (9).

The contrast between Pope and Horace persists. Pitiful "Hunc" (7), a spendthrift, looted only his own estate in order to buy expensive food, but Con. Philips devours the substance of her "Cullies" (15). Roman Fufidius, a miser (of course) and an avaricious, unprincipled moneylender, is harsh to his debtors, vile in diligently seeking out naive young men to accept his usurious loans (12–17), but he avoids the excesses of Pope's Fufidia (Lady Mary). She "turns her very Sister to a Job" (21). Like Fufidius, she lives poorly despite her wealth ("Yet starves herself" [23]), but in addition suffers from a sexual mania (24).

What causes such perverse behavior? Horace blames the foolish extremism he mocks on an understandable motive: concern for what others think. Of course, one should care about one's good name, as he reminds us (58–59), but without being driven into folly by the fear of a bad reputation. We are not expressly told that this affected Tigellius, but the tightwad who neglects his friend fears the label "prodigus," the epicure "sordidus," and the hustling Fufidius "vappae famam . . . ac nebulonis" (4, 10, 12) ("a reputation as a wastrel or a bum"). Pope's women, however, have no similar concerns. Perhaps the most frightening thing about them is their lack of any reason for the things they do. They simply act upon their instincts, which are destructive.

The appearance of monsters who lack motives betokens a monstrous, illogical world, which continues to reveal its nature after line 38. In contrast, Horace's world makes sense. It is reasonable that adulterers should suffer (the main theme in the *sermo*), and that they too should suffer who lose their senses over promiscuous unmarried women (a secondary theme). Firm standards exist, and they are not exclusively "shalt nots." To Horace, expressing himself in a style once disdained as "grossly Roman,"[16] one wise course is sex with a whore; the prudent client need fear no furious husbands and, in addition, has the opportunity to examine the "togata" undressed before paying (80–85). Horace is much less

enthusiastic about amateur sluts, but a conservative spender
should do well with them too (49–53). For sudden impulses, ser-
vants are handy, whether female or male:

> . . . tument tibi cum inguina, num, si
> Ancilla aut verna est praesto puer, impetus in quem
> Continuo fiat, malis tentigine rumpi?

> (116–18)

> (. . . so when your member swells, if you have
> a serving girl convenient, or serving boy, to satisfy
> the impulse on the spot, why endure a prick about to blow?)

Even the rakish speaker of *Sober Advice* has trouble with
Horace's practical perspective on sex. The imitation comes close in
one brief endorsement of whoring (161–66) and when developing
the relatively innocuous point (in 108–11 and 133–36) that a pros-
titute "shows what Ware she has to sell" (109). It departs from the
source elsewhere on the topic of satisfactory sex, and in doing so,
strangely enough, suggests that the contemporary world is less, not
more, firmly governed by moral standards than was lewd old Rome.

This is true of lines 39–44, which render the Latin 31–35, on
going to brothels. There Horace quotes Cato's pompous but approving words ("'macte / Virtute esto'" [32]) to a young man who visits
one rather than "'grinding'" ("'Permolere'" [35]) others' wives.
But in the English at this point we read not of a naturally libidinous
youth, but of a "*noted Dean* much busy'd in the Park" (40). And
"My Lord," by whom Pope meant the Bishop of London, encourages this frolic with a wild enthusiasm that makes Cato's approval
look even staider: "'Proceed (he cry'd) proceed, my Reverend
Brother, / ' 'Tis *Fornicatio simplex,* and no other'" (41–42). "My
Lord" does disapprove of adultery, although another "my Lord,"
an archbishop, is said to engage in that, and of "lust[ing] for Boys,
with *Pope* and *Turk*" (43–44). Nonetheless, the wide gap between a
young man fornicating where fornicating is appropriate and the
Dean rutting in the open air implies, at the least, that Britain lacks
firm standards for sex.[17]

"Hic" in line 49 below stands as another good example which
Horace believes all should follow.

> Tutior at quanto merx est in classe secunda!
> Libertinarum dico: Sallustius in qua
> Non minus insanit, quam qui moechatur. at hic si,
> Qua res, qua ratio sauderet [*in error for* suaderet], quaque modeste

Munifico esse licet, vellet bonus atque benignus
Esse; daret quantum satis esset, nec sibi damno
Dedecorique foret.

(47–53)

(But the second class stuff isn't necessarily safer,
freedwomen, I mean, over whom Sallustius goes crazy,
no less so than the stud who chases wives. But if moved
as good sense and economy direct, to temper munificence
with moderation, as he should, a man desired to be both
generous and right, he'd give what is enough, not unseemly
and a waste.)

"Hic" might be Sallustius, who makes a fool of himself with
vulgar women [48–49], but could do better. As I understand it,
"hic" is more general, "a man" (delayed for two lines in my translation): anyone could do better if moved by reason. But Pope's "S——
st," the subject of the whole passage, seems by contrast irredeema-
bly wrong-headed:

And yet some Care of S——st should be had,
Nothing so mean for which he can't run mad;
His Wit confirms him but a Slave the more,
And makes a Princess whom he found a Whore.
The Youth might save much Trouble and Expence,
Were he a Dupe of only common Sense.

(63–68)

The stress falls on the folly, not the possibility of correction. Moreover, the "Wit" of this Sallust, instead of having the capacity to lead
him aright, only prods him on to greater follies. Without wit, we are
told, he might be better off, but even dullness would not deliver
him, as a "Dupe of only common Sense," to the happily moderate
condition of his counterpart in *Sat.* 1.2. Obviously he is unable to
follow the Horatian standards of "good sense and economy."

In lines 47–60 Pope shows adulterers being punished. So adultery
is wrong. But how difficult it is to know what is right! Prostitution
has possibilities, but does not receive the recommendation Cato
gives it. There is always marriage, unmentioned in the Latin, but
marriage is mocked by a parody of St. Paul: why, "when a tight,
neat Girl, will serve the Turn, / In errant Pride continue stiff, and
burn?" (151–52).[18] Nor is the couplet a firmly rakish endorsement
of fornication. Here tightness and neatness suggest, to me at least,
an uncomfortable, dry kind of sexual friction, while "burn," which

suggests that the speaker laughs at Paul, also makes us think of venereal disease. In addition, the lack of any hint of Horace's casual acceptance of convenient homosexuality in the lines imitated (116–18), as the "tight, neat Girl" takes the place of Horace's convenient servant of either sex, lends a prudish air.

In view of the uncertainty in which the average male sensualist must dwell, perhaps we feel that adulterers deserve the sympathy that, as Atkins notes, the imitation gives them.[19] It appears less in the speaker's expressions of pity than in the punishments the poem shows them enduring (47–60), considerably less drastic than those enthusiastically described in the Latin 37–46. This may be consoling, and it makes the imitation's world less horrifying in one respect than Horace's, instead of more so. But it is not consoling to reflect that this mildness signifies a society that knows no right way.

Something has surely gone wrong with the people in this disordered place. Accordingly, through contrasts with Horace, Pope suggests that man receives no guidance from nature.

To Ofellus, we recall, nature is a great embracing order within which he instinctively knows his part: nature also plays a part in him. In this satire Horace assumes a similar presence of nature in us, allied with the *animus,* or reason. Although false ideas, based on what we think others think, can confuse us, we have an innate capacity to act rightly. Thus in his lines 68–72, Horace suggests the union of reason and appetite in an image appropriate to his subject, for he imagines the "animus" of an adulterer as the spokesman for his penis, "mutonis verbis . . . / Diceret haec animus . . ." (68–69) ("speaking for the prick. . . . / the mind . . ."). Neither, they jointly protest, values in the least the high birth of the noblewoman that impresses their foolish master. In Pope's equivalent 87–95, "that honest Part that rules us all" (87) is made to "rise" without cooperation from the reason, and it speaks only for itself.

When Horace explicitly mentions and somewhat personifies *natura,* he presents her as an inner presence. She will guide us, if we let her, and she thrives or suffers according to how we treat ourselves:

> At quanto meliora monet, pugnantiaque istis
> Dives opis natura suae! tu si modo recte
> Dispensare velis, ac non fugienda petendis
> Inmiscere.
>
> (73–76)

(But nature, who has a special store of riches, will guide you better and in quite another way, if only you would choose

to be a wiser manager and not confuse desirable goods
with those you should avoid.)

> Nonne, cupidinibus statuat natura modum quem,
> Quid latura, sibi quid sit dolitura negatum,
> Quaerere plus prodest.

(111–13)

(Ask nature what boundaries she sets to passion, what she needs
for herself, what, if denied, hurts her—these questions
are useful.)

The passages in *Sober Advice* equivalent to these indicate that
nature sets limits, "bounds to wild Desire" (143), which men vio-
late, just as they do in the *sermo*. However, Pope's nature is not an
inner presence eager to guide us, but a great frame, a "stupendous
whole," as the imitation's version of Horace's 73–75 makes clear:[20]

> Hath not indulgent Nature spread a Feast,
> And giv'n enough for Man, enough for Beast?
> But Man corrupt, perverse in all his ways,
> In search of Vanities from Nature strays:
> Yea, tho' the Blessing's more than he can use,
> Shuns the permitted, the forbid pursues!

(96–101)

Here nature lies only without, and returning to our proper place in
her order—after the straying, for which the suddenly moral rake
reproaches us—seems a harder task than allowing Horace's nature,
lying both without and within, to guide us: the latter requires only
choosing "to be a better manager" of oneself. Contemplating "Man
corrupt, perverse in all his ways," the imitation does not echo
Horace's encouragement to make this choice.

Pope's lines 143–46, his rendering of the second Latin passage
quoted above, ignore Horace's assumption that nature, dwelling
within us, suffers or thrives according to the choices we make. We
are indeed reminded that she has given us "Sense to guide," and
"Reason to enquire" (144), but nature lies without, and our ability
to play our proper role there appears particularly tenuous because
of the contrast with nature in this *sermo*. Compared to Horace's
description of unnatural behavior, Pope's judgment exposes a separation between man and nature that threatens to be permanent.

Pope leaves us in doubt all the greater because Horace has none.
Reading *Sober Advice,* we doubt the access to the fund of good

sense, the nature within, that Horace assumes everyone possesses. We doubt the value of codes thought to control sex and even, because of the speaker's occasional hesitancy, the liberation that sex is thought to bring. We may even doubt—especially when we compare the two beginnings—our understanding of what a human being is.

Pope's forays here into the unnatural in shape and action do not represent his final judgment on humanity; it would be interesting to compare this imitation with book 4 of *The Dunciad*. But obviously *Sober Advice from Horace* reveals his concern that the world is falling away from an orderly condition. The norm for order, despite the abundant folly Horace puts on view, is the world of *Sat. 1.2.*

As I have pointed out, that world makes sense. Therefore, satire makes sense. Horace's criticism of extremists and adulterers should have some effect, in a society with standards, on fools in whom a kind nature continues to dwell and in whom reason and passion prefer to cooperate. Pope can count on nothing similar. He does not, in fact, say very much about what lustful men should do, rather than not do. For what desirable condition, then, is his satire attempting to reclaim them? And how can they be reached, if they and nature are so greatly out of touch? *Sober Advice* is certainly serious satire, as are the other *Imitations of Horace*—no less serious because, like them, it implies that satire is futile.

7

Refuge in a Toppling World

An Epistle to Dr. Arbuthnot

Although traditionally associated with the *Imitations of Horace,* the *Epistle to Dr. Arbuthnot* is not an imitation, for it follows no single Horatian text. Certainly Pope alludes to various poems and poets, but the kind of comparative study I have been making is not possible. Hence, I here intend only a brief survey of two themes in this satire that are also significant in the *Imitations.*

Such a survey would lack point if Horace were not an important presence in this nonimitation, but no one doubts that he is. Although I do not agree with the traditional estimate that the "metaphor of the poem is quite simply 'Horace',"[1] he may be somewhat more present for me than for other contemporary critics of *Arbuthnot.* I would say, for example, that the Bufo portrait alludes to Horace's Nasidienus, in *Sat.* 2.8, as much as to the patron in Juvenal's seventh satire.[2] Of course, both allusions may come together in our minds. More important than either, however, is the opposition between Bufo and Maecenas, whom we think of when Pope says of Bufo, "*Horace* and he went hand in hand in song" (234).

Nor, to give another instance, should the portrait of Sporus seem exclusively Juvenalian simply because Pope is very angry, or be considered "unlike anything in Horace."[3] This "Amphibious Thing" (326) is related to the category of fools Horace considered most foolish, those who rush from one extreme to its opposite: "Veering away from one vice, fools collide with its contrary" (*Sat.* 1.2.24). Although Horace merely laughs at Tigellius, for example, because "he was extreme in everything" (*Sat.* 1.3.9), this individual could very well be one of the antecedents for Sporus, "His Wit all see-saw between *that* and *this,* / Now high, now low, now Master up, now Miss" (323–24).[4]

But we need not argue about the extent of the allusion. It is certainly reasonable to think of Horace while reading Pope's *Ar-*

93

buthnot. More to the point, we can accept the possibility that it develops certain themes present in the *Imitations of Horace* written earlier and which later *Imitations* continue to develop. These are the status of Twickenham as a refuge, to be considered first, and the present state of literary patronage. Comparison with Horace's life and work suggests how serious are the consequences of Twickenham's breaching, of patronage's failure.

The lesser order, its security not entirely credible in the imitation of *Sat* 2.2, can now be penetrated. "All fly to *Twit'nam*" (21), all would-be poets, and pass through every barrier including the door, which politeness allows Pope to shut only when it is almost true for his servant to say, of him, "I'm sick, I'm dead" (2). Obviously Pope overdoes it: the siege of Twickenham is a bit of mock-epic that, by causing us to laugh at poor Pope while letting us know he shares the joke, allows us to feel ourselves allied with him, the man of wit, against the dull world. However, despite the exaggeration, we sense a serious truth in Pope's vision of the invading dunces; they are a concrete expression of the world's power to vex him, and vexing Pope is not a trivial offense. Further on, he emphasizes that poetry is his vocation: "As yet a Child, nor yet a Fool to Fame, / I lisp'd in Numbers, for the Numbers came" (127–28). It is his destiny, God-given, with which the dunces interfere.

What drives them? Certainly no similar destiny, not even a modest talent. Hoping to join the newly evolved occupational class of hacks, they seek his influence with players and printers, but even this seems a minor interest. Moreover, they do not consciously intend Pope any harm. Behind their invasion lies a force, allied to madness ("All *Bedlam, or Parnassus,* is let out" [4]), that Pope does not claim to understand. Only with hindsight can one recognize the dunces as devotees of Goddess Dulness, members of her final company. *Arbuthnot,* however, does identify the breakdowns in culture that help make these creatures what they are.

The tradition of craft has failed: Pope's Horatian "saving counsel, 'Keep your Piece nine years',," stirs, not outrage, but simple incomprehension: "Nine years! cries he" (40–41). No one cares or knows anything about the classics, a point apparent in the compliments of those "who to my Person pay their court" (115) and pretend to see the classical tradition made manifest in coughs, eyes, uneven shoulders, inclinations of the head (116–24). Critic-pedants infest literature, devoted to "comma's and points" (161). Pope emphasizes one further reason more than any other: the decline of patronage, an institution that, at its best, upheld standards by supporting true poets, has obviously helped to turn the literary world over to hordes of careerists.

We are reminded that "great George," who "scorns the Poet's Lays" in the imitation of *Sat.* 2.1, never heeds his "Birth-day Song" (222) and would not, even if it were good. A faulty critic because of his moral nature, Atticus also fails as a patron, since he misuses his power to affect writers' careers. Bufo is anti-Maecenas, the noble patron as buffoon, and Sporus is another kind of failed patron: in a properly run state, a man in his position would have supported deserving poets. Instead, he opposes Pope.

Sporus is also a source of undefined national malaise: squatting at the "Ear of *Eve*" (Queen Caroline), he "spits himself abroad" (319–20), infecting everything. In him Pope clearly indicates a significant connection between the decline of literary patronage and that of England as a whole. The same point seems apparent in the lines on George and on Bufo, the debased aristocrat, and it is suggested by the portrait of Atticus, described as an unjust literary lawgiver and ruler. By attacking these figures, Pope shows a characteristic concern for his nation's well-being.

However, in a poem indeed conspicuous for its "uncertainty" or sense of "unresolved debate,"[5] he seems unaccountably to forget both this broader concern and the swarms of bad poets he shows disturbing him at Twickenham. Reversing the security-to-insecurity pattern of the first of the *Imitations,* late in *Arbuthnot* Pope claims to possess "a Poet's Dignity and Ease" (263). Similarly, while he blesses the Bufos of the world (255) for their willingness to "receiv[e] of Wits an undistinguish'd race," who are thus "whistled off my hands" (237, 254), we might wonder how the "undistinguish'd race" could harass any man more.

He is equally self-contradictory when considering the plight of other true poets. Just as the first of the *Imitations* implies that George's contempt for verse actually protects Pope, so does *Arbuthnot* observe that "*Dryden* alone (what wonder?) came not nigh" Bufo (245), and that the class of Bufos, preoccupied with the bad poets who justly receive poor rewards, "left me [Pope] Gay" (256). Pope's immediate afterthoughts, however, dissipate whatever comfort we find in the idea that good poets somehow repel bad patrons. While Dryden escaped Bufo, no good patron took his place; Bufo "help'd to bury whom he help'd to starve." And in Gay Pope sadly saw "neglected Genius bloom, / Neglected die!" (247, 257–58).

Now, Rome's Augustan Age provides celebrated examples both

of retirement and of patronage, and on these subjects Horace is the most approachable Augustan source. Though not an imitation, *An Epistle to Dr. Arbuthnot* shows Pope applying Horace's poetry in rather general fashion to his own world and his position in it. It is probable that *Arbuthnot* lacks coherence partly because, although Pope lays claim to that "Poet's Dignity and Ease" one can rightly think of as Horatian, he must recognize the major differences between Horace's situation and his own.

Horace had power. Pope is polite to the dunces who besiege him, more so that Horace would have been, and he seems in this way to maintain Horatian "animus aequus." His politeness, however, may be less a sign of a balanced soul than of a sense of weakness that comes from being alone, unsupported by the great. Similarly, when Pope forsakes politeness and ease to rail at Sporus, we can reasonably infer that this same underlying weakness is frustrating him into rage. With Arbuthnot, we question Pope's ability to cause " 'that Thing of silk' " any pain: " '. . . can *Sporus* feel?' " (305, 307).

More specifically, Horace had patrons. Of course, although Pope lacks them, John Gay's fate will not be his; but patronage can mean more than financial support. We are reminded of what it means to Horace by lines 135–46, which, as Butt's note points out (p. 105), allude to *Sat.* 1.10.81–90; here Horace enumerates the great men who favor him, it is important to note, at the time of writing. By their patronage, they include him among Rome's ruling circle. In contrast, Pope's parallel list refers to the past, to his very early career; all, even Bolingbroke, are classed among "great *Dryden's* friends before" (141). Obviously he valued the respect and friendship of "*Granville* the polite," "knowing *Walsh,* "Courtly *Talbot*" (135, 136, 139), and the others; these should have been the ruling circle. At any rate, Pope has no such circle to support him now, and the comparison with Horace's situation stresses his isolation and powerlessness.

Pope has no patrons now and needs none simply in order to live, but it would be a mistake to conclude that the failure of patrons, as a class, properly to value poets and poetry does not affect him. First, they are partly responsible for the hordes unleashed upon Twickenham: for, that is, the disturbing influence of the new, mercenary mode of literary production, unchecked by any traditional support for true poets, upon the man who appears to be the last true poet. Second, the failure of those in power to be good patrons reflects their failure to lead in other ways; therefore, Pope must oppose them because they neglect their traditional responsibilities, not just to poets, but to the nation as a whole.

This he must do without allies. Only the aging Arbuthnot remains on Pope's side, it would seem, and he is a correspondent, not a guest. In the first two *Imitations,* Pope had company he valued. Hence there was more "Ease" in those poems and more hope too. In *Arbuthnot,* dramatizing forces rather than reporting facts, Pope shows himself entertaining no one at Twickenham, not even the weary old friends of his version of *Sat.* 2.2. Compared to Horace, living in the single order of the Empire, always at the center of things no matter how far geographically removed from Rome, he appears particularly isolated. Compared to Horace's powerful projection in most of the *sermones* of his own serenity, Pope's claims for peace of mind at Twickenham seem hollow and sad.

The Second Epistle of the Second Book of Horace, Imitated

In 1737 Pope imitated *Epist.* 2.2, in which we encounter the poet Horace with both the Odes and book 1 of the Epistles behind him, ready to retire in the fullness of age and honors. Now Pope implicitly compares himself with the official, "Augustan" eminence. We can anticipate an increased sense of the difference between the two, one speaking so authoritatively for those in power, the other so fiercely against them. The difference may help to account for much of the imitation's anger and for its apocalyptic satire, both of which are most prominent in its grandest passage, lines 212–63.

Perhaps I should begin by saying that Pope's confronting the "Augustan" Horace certainly does not mean his turning toward the revisionist version of Horace as an imperial lackey. We see no evidence of this, even though Pope had a great opportunity in the very first line, where Horace addresses the epistle's recipient, Julius Florus: "Flore, bono claroque fidelis amice Neroni" ("Dear Florus, noble, good Tiberius's faithful friend"). Florus's friend, Tiberius Claudius Nero, would become the second emperor; thoroughly unattractive to later centuries, he was "bonus clarusque" to Horace, who, Pope could have reminded us, served the man who delivered Rome to Tiberius and the monsters who succeeded him. But Pope ignores his chance, although he might have used it to present himself, through contrast with Horace, as a defender of freedom.

He makes, in fact, a considerable effort to liken himself to Horace. The most striking sign of his intention occurs in the imitation's autobiographical passage (52–71). Lacking the university edu-

cation equivalent to the period of instruction in Athens where
Horace learned "*curvo* dignoscere *rectum*" (44) ("to tell the
crooked from the straight"), he introduces his father, who "taught
me from a Lad, / The better Art to know the good from bad" (54–
55). Horace does not discuss his own father in this *sermo* (except
for a reference to losing his "paternal" inheritance [50]), but does so
elsewhere with great affection and respect, and with particular
gratitude for his excellence as a moral teacher.[6]

When Pope declares, "I live and thrive, / Indebted to no Prince or
Peer alive" (68–69), he may be indicating that he is better than
Horace, because of his independence. However, the suggestion
would be somewhat clearer if, in the passage imitated, lines 49–54,
Horace referred to Augustus or Maecenas; instead, he says only
that now, no longer poor, he no longer needs to write. Nor does
Pope manipulate the context of his own passage to bring out the
contrast between Horace's client status and his own situation.
Finally, when for his present freedom from want he gives "thanks to
Homer" (68), he may allude to Horace, whose Odes resemble
Pope's translation in being an assimilation of Greek art into the
poet's own tongue.

Pope's most extended effort to appear Horatian is his conclusion
(284–327), which presents the poet as a composed and philosophic
soul, calmly awaiting death. The Latin epistle does approximately
this in its 190–216, and Pope's lines seem, to me at least, closer to
free translation than to imitation. We should consider, however, the
question of whether they resolve certain troubling issues, relating
to his goals as a poet and as a man, raised earlier in the poem. For if
these issues are not resolved, the Horatian image with which it
ends becomes a mere pose, perhaps a rather desperate one.

According to recent critics—who mention distinctions between
the two endings without denying their general similarity—Pope
resolves all issues, all tensions, very well. He achieves a final
personal "dignity and grace," or something perhaps similar, "ma-
ture self-knowledge," or something larger, an acceptance of "universal concord and . . . justice."[7] My interpretation differs. *The
Second Epistle of the Second Book of Horace, Imitated* exposes
more fully than any previous imitation the great distance between
what Pope wants for himself and what the world will give him.
When source and imitation are compared, he will be seen as uncer-
tain whether to persist in his satiric war against those in power or to
enter a philosophical retirement that, however, seems to assure him
neither a peaceful nor a virtuous existence.

Aubrey L. Williams first explored the significance of Pope's use of thievery in this poem as a "controlling metaphor" that becomes prominent, through contrast, because Horace does not employ it. Other critics have subsequently considered the gaps contributing to this effect.[8] But another class of gaps, which seem no less evident, has received much less attention—a curious thing in view of the recent tendency to emphasize the political content in Pope's work. Through differing from *Epist.* 2.2, Pope strengthens his imitation's attack on court and king and on established power in general.

While one does not need Horace to realize that the political satire exists, several illustrations will show that Pope's sallies derive much of their force and point from the contrast with the Latin. Thus in lines 135–46, which show poets complimenting one another, although "Laurel Crowns" (142) and a few other references suggest a sneer at the king, a contrast with the *sermo* confirms and develops the allusion. The Horatian passage (91–101) also mentions figurative crowns woven of mutual compliments (96), but the allusion to kings stops there; in fact, although self-importance afflicts Horace's poets, they have no regal airs at all, and so the English poets seem even more pretentious and arrogant.

The reader of the Latin epistle is politely asked to enter the library and listen to the complimenting—if he has time: "si forte vacas" (95). But Pope—pretending, like Horace, to be of this doltish company—regally commands: "Walk with respect behind" (141). Then Horace compares his buffoons to the slowest of gladiators, heavily armored Samnites (a turn the imitation omits), exchanging awkward buffets of praise (97–98). Finally, like good Republicans, the poets in the epistle cast their votes: "Discedo Alcaeus puncto illius; ille meo quis?" (99) ("His ballot makes me Alcaeus; and mine makes him?"). In the imitation their equivalents knight one another: ". . . allow me *Dryden's* strains, / And you shall rise up *Otway* for your pains" (145–46). Given the setting of Merlin's Cave, the library established by Queen Caroline, readers should find it easy to think not just of kings, but of George, and to consider him no more authentically royal than these poseurs are poetic.

In addition, Pope aims a thrust at the judiciary through a gap between the beginnings of the two poems. Horace, arguing that Florus has no right to demand a letter or a poem from him after being told that he would not and could not write, enforces his point with a vignette concerning a slave-dealer (2–19). Presented dramatically, as if speaking to a prospective customer, this character praises a slave he has for sale, but admits that once he ran away.

Thus the buyer is properly informed. If the slave should flee, Horace says, legal action against the dealer would be unjust, just as Florus's demands are unjust. The courts would support the dealer: "Ille ferat pretium, poena securus" (17) ("He could take your money and not be penalized"). The law supports what is right. But Pope cites a case of judge and justice going astray. If his correspondent, demanding verse, "should prosecute,"

> I think Sir Godfrey should decide the Suit;
> Who sent the Thief that stole the Cash, away,
> And punish'd him that put it in his way.
>
> (24–26)

Pope also attacks men of rank in general. His example of a man deluded but content is a Member of Parliament who took part in imaginary debates (184–97), compared to Horace's Argive playgoer who applauded imaginary plays (128–40). In the crowded London streets—"dehumanizing," as Bogel says—those dehumanized are men of rank from two different social classes.[9] "Aldermen" argue precedence with an ass, and "Peers give way" to their own excrement in a "Carr" (105–7). In his 72–75 Horace has wagons, a pig, and a dog, but no important men; and therefore their presence, like that of the hallucinating "worthy Member" (185), signifies Pope's animus against the establishment.

In the speech of the Frenchman who takes the slave-dealer's place, Pope uses a contrast with Horace to mock the very idea of "Honour," to which all the dignitaries he attacks can be expected to give much lip service. Seeking a place for his son, the Frenchman declines to praise the boy too highly because " 'To say too much, might do my Honour wrong' " (12). His Horatian counterpart considers himself a plain businessman and claims only that he can afford to tell the truth:

> "Multa fidem promissa levant, ubi plenius aequo
> "Laudet venales, qui vult extrudere, merces.
> "Res urget me nulla: meo sum pauper in aere."
>
> (10–12)

("Big promises won't build your confidence; when men praise
too heavily what they sell, they're trying to get rid of it.
But not me, I don't have to; I'm poor, but I don't owe.")

Both men present obvious sales pitches; the dealer, at least, avoids sinking to the aristocratic pretentions Pope mocks.

The court of Augustus comes into the picture, as a norm, in Pope's rendering of Horace's 109–14. Describing the exemplary poet's role as a linguistic *censor* (110), Horace insists that words which lack dignity or clear meaning must not be used, even if they have lingered "intra penetralia Vestae" (114) ("in Vesta's temple")—have, that is, ancient and holy associations. But in the imitation the poet should not use an unsuitable word "tho' at Court (perhaps) it may find grace" (162). Horace has no worries about the language used at his court, and, considering his relationship with Augustus and Maecenas, one's understanding of the imitation may include the contrast between the Augustan court supporting the censor-poet and George's court that degrades language (and other things), thus compelling the true poet to act as *its* censor.

Horace is allied to power; Pope attacks it in his satire and shows us that he has good reason. However, early in the imitation he reminds his correspondent, the "Col'nel," that "I told you when I went, I could not write" (28). Then, at line 198, he expands on this decision:

> Well, on the whole, *plain* Prose must be my fate:
> Wisdom (curse on it) will come soon or late.
> There is a time when Poets will grow dull:
> I'll e'en leave Verses to the Boys at school.
>
> (198–201)

At this point we are told that he intends to fill the place of poetry with philosophy and learn to "keep the equal Measure of the Soul" (205). The "Verses" surely include satire, which would agitate the "equal Measure," and yet a satiric temper forces its way into his meditations, as will be seen. Moreover, philosophic retirement, perhaps none too peaceful, perhaps none too moral, appears a dubious alternative to writing satire.

Pope wants peace, but retirement may not afford him that. In 206–22 he pictures himself "all alone" (210) in his country home, where he sits philosophizing. Earlier, however, he hints that he may not often be left there all alone and undisturbed, whether attempting to write or think. Even when he appears to praise rural retirement, certain lines arouse our doubts, especially if we compare them to their Latin equivalents. Such, for example, are 110–13, based on Horace's 77–78. After ruling out frenetic Rome as a place for writing, Horace remarks: "Scriptorum chorus omnis *amat nemus, & fugit urbes, / Rite cliens Bacchi, somno gaudentis &*

umbra" ("The whole poetic chorus loves the groves and flees the city, / good followers of Bacchus, who delights in sleep and shade"). Although this is by no means solemn, Pope, who ironically includes himself in the chorus, angles his version toward the absurd:

> Alas! to Grotto's and to Groves we run.
> To Ease and Silence, ev'ry Muse's Son:
> *Blackmore* himself, for any grand Effort,
> Would drink and doze at *Tooting* or *Earl's-Court.*

How long can "Ease and Silence" survive? By naming these abstractions, Pope reminds us of their fragility and leads us to wonder about the effect on them of a galloping mob of poets; for "run" replaces "fugit," a term conveying no clear picture. Moreover, the imitation's poets merely "run," while the epistle's "chorus" goes to something it "loves." This gap may seem minor, but by making the English poets seem a mindless herd, it leads us to associate them with the dunces who storm Twickenham in the *Epistle to Dr. Arbuthnot.* "To Grotto's" also resounds for readers of that poem, remembering ". . . thro' my Grot they glide," especially since Horace has only "groves" ("nemus"). Another difference between the two poems here is the presence of Pope's Bacchus, Blackmore, associated with noise in the first *Imitation;* there Sir Richard is "rumbling, rough and fierce"; here he reposes at "Tooting."

But let us assume that Pope can achieve a peaceful life. What should he do with it? Beginning at line 198 he applies to his own circumstances Horace's decision "non verba sequi fidibus modulanda Latinis" (143) ("to look no more for words that fit the Latin lyre") and to begin the study of philosophy. But Pope varies from his model in predicting that "*plain* Prose must be my fate" (198). This seems inauthentic somehow, compared to Horace's vow to swear off writing lyric poetry only; Horace intended, in all probability, to continue with "philosophizing epistles" like *Epist.* 2.2 itself.[10] Does Pope mean he will write only letters to friends? If so, why is this very letter in verse? At any rate, readers may scent ambiguity and a revocable quality about the decision to take up philosophy. They may also be made suspicious by the inwardness of Pope's philosophical regimen, a quality that becomes apparent if we contrast the equivalent English and Latin passages.

Rather than write lyric poetry, Horace intends "*verae numerosque modosque* ediscere *vitae*" (144) ("to learn the notes and rhythms of real life"). Instead of "real life," I might have translated "verae . . . vitae" as "true life," in order to suggest a pondering of the ideal; for "real life" pushes us toward the world, toward Rome and away from what might seem to be the proper subjects of meditation. However, even though his home is in the country and his pursuits philosophical, Horace does not divorce himself from Rome. C. W. Macleod ably explains what philosophy meant to him:

> . . . the poet's philosophical detachment does not cause him to look down with pity or contempt on other people; he tries rather to see what all men, and what each individual, needs in order to live well, and to share his insight with his readers so that they can use it in their own way.[11]

Now, to the Latin "Ac non verba sequi fidibus modulanda Latinis, / Sed *verae numerosque modosque* ediscere *vitae*," let us compare the imitation's 202–5:

> To Rules of Poetry no more confin'd,
> I learn to smooth and harmonize my Mind,
> Teach ev'ry Thought within its bounds to roll,
> And keep the equal Measure of the Soul.

Despite "learn," there is no sense of learning *from* anyone or anything; moreover, Pope intends to "teach" not practical wisdom to others or even to himself, but a lesson of restraint to his own thoughts. He seems to care for nothing outside of himself. His theme is a final adjusting of the spirit and a turning away from the world; since those who hold power in it seem incapable of being instructed, turning away seems reasonable, and one usually commends any effort to achieve inner harmony. And yet, compared to Horace's intention for himself, the course proposed in these lines seems narrow, almost selfish. While nothing ironic in the passage's language suggests that Pope really rejects it, I sense a questioning and a lack of dedication.

Finally, philosophizing threatens to move Pope into a despised category within the poem, as in Pope's work generally—those bound up in self. These include the deluded legislator, happiest in an empty House when imagining himself a great statesman (Horace's theatergoer applauds others, if imaginary others) and the scholar even more withdrawn, "So stiff, so mute!" (121), than Horace's "Ingenium" (81). Similarly, while Rome's bad poets "laudant quidquid scripsere" ("praise whatever they've composed"), presumably aloud, if others are silent ("Si taceas") (108), when "all mankind reject" Britain's "bad Rhimers" (153), they fall ecstatically

mute: "Each prais'd within, is happy all day long" (156). Pope's
personal goals as he states them—the limiting of thought, the con-
centration on self—hint at a similar self-involvement and so reflect
on the virtue of retirement.

Lines 206–11 appear, I admit, perfectly sincere:

> Soon as I enter at my Country door,
> My Mind resumes the thread it dropt before;
> Thoughts, which at Hyde-Park-Corner I forgot,
> Meet and rejoin me, in the pensive Grott.
> There all alone, and Compliments apart,
> I ask these sober questions of my heart.

Therefore Bogel, after noting that Pope understands—in the case of
the scholar, for example—how "retirement can readily come to
mean limitation," reasonably claims that a final "harmony begins
to take shape in Pope's picture of his own retirement" in lines 206–
11.[12] An *inner* harmony, that is, seems possible for Pope, no matter
what the world does.

I would say, however, that these lines make that harmony seem
only possible, not probable, since Pope has previously hinted at
quite serious limitations upon his proposed retirement. One should
mistrust the harmonizing power of the "Thoughts" which "Meet
and rejoin me, in the pensive Grott" if Pope intends only to "Teach
ev'ry Thought within its bounds to roll." And, in fact, the forthcom-
ing meditation he promises on the "sober questions" he will ask his
heart does not occur. There is little inwardness in the following
lines, 212–63. His thoughts roll, or pierce, far beyond their bounds,
as Pope bursts into satire against the rich and high-placed, then
rises to a towering denunciation of mankind, and finally concludes
the passage with a vision of all-embracing death.

The Latin lines equivalent to Pope's 212–63, it is important to
realize, *are* philosophy—intended, of course, for the reader. The
Latin 146–79 show Horace working hard, if gracefully, to instruct;
the only satire this passage contains is restrained mockery of a
landowner who fails to understand the lack of any practical difference between owning a farm and merely buying the farm products that one needs. We are in the world of "vera vita." The
purpose of the poet whom William S. Anderson has called the
"Roman Socrates" is to have us question ourselves about the value
we place on wealth and property.[13] His instruments are, first, comparisons between physical and moral health, and, second, the

theme of land ownership versus use (*dominium* versus *ususfructus*).

Pope begins by accurately rendering Horace's 146–48 with his 212–15. If we cannot satisfy our thirst, both say, we call a doctor; and so, if no amount of wealth can satisfy you, "nulline faterier audes?" (148) ("do you dare not confess that illness?"), or: ". . . why not with equal ease / Confess as well your Folly, as Disease?" (214–15). But Pope's 216–17, based on nothing in the epistle, turn this helpful question into the deceptive prelude to a sneer, for there exists another answer besides the "of course we must" that Horace hopes will be given: "The Heart resolves this matter in a trice, / 'Men only feel the Smart, but not the Vice.'" Men respond only to pain, to punishment, and cannot act before it is too late.

The Latin lines 149–57, equivalent to the imitation's 218–29, use the metaphor of a wound and the medicinal root or herb, which, when it fails to cure the wound, we cease applying. So if, though richer, we are no wiser, how can we go on taking the world's bad advice that those to whom "Rem Di donarent, illi decedere pravam / Stultitiam" (152–53) ("the gods give riches are freed from evil / foolishness")? Pope, however, turns this bit of sermonizing into a satire upon his customary targets—the court and the nobility, along with a degraded, "servile" clergy:

> When golden Angels cease to cure the Evil,
> You give all royal Witchcraft to the Devil:
> When servile Chaplains cry, that Birth and Place
> Indue a Peer with Honour, Truth, and Grace,
> Look in that Breast, most dirty Duke! be fair,
> Say, can you find out one such Lodger there?
> Yet still, not heeding what your Heart can teach,
> You go to Church to hear these Flatt'rers preach.
>
> (218–25)

In its anger, the attack sacrifices some clarity. What can his heart teach the Duke if in his breast he finds no virtues? Horace is teaching without flattering; Pope assaults.

It is true that in his treatment of ownership versus use Pope assumes the same reasonable reader that Horace does: one who owns no farm but lives as well, Pope says, as he who "bought at thousands, what with better wit / You purchase as you want, and bit by bit" (236–37). However, his satire of the landowner is both more specific and more dire. In place of the generalized "Emtor" (167) (the buyer of land), Pope supplies "Worldly" (234) (that is, Wortley Montagu), Gilbert Heathcote (240), and "vile Van-Muck" (229) (for Vanneck, who wanted to buy Bolingbroke's Dawley Farm). These specimens exemplify the class of "large-acred Men" (240) who in covetousness outstrip Horace's representative Roman landowner, greedy but willing to accept boundaries established by the wise laws of a wise state:

> Sed *vocat* usque *suum,* qua populus adsita certis
> Limitibus vicina refugit jurgia.
>
> (170–71)

> (But he calls his all before the poplar on the line
> that keeps him out of battles with the neighbors.)

In contrast, Pope renders these lines with a couplet that, by referring vaguely to a boundary halfway into the distance, stresses not limits to greed, but how far greed extends. It also establishes a parallel between the "large-acred Men" and the devil: "Yet these are Wights, who fondly call their own / Half that the Dev'l o'erlooks from Lincoln Town" (244–45).

Of course, the idea of owning land will seem foolish to anyone who has taken to heart Horace's *Sat.* 2.2, in which Ofellus, that master of *"verae numerosque modosque . . . vitae,"* explains that the land has no owners. *Epist.* 2.2.171–74 restates that thesis, and in his 246–51 Pope renders its essential sense. However, in the twelve lines that follow he goes against both the sense and style of his model, and by doing so strongly impresses us with his mood of violent despair.

On the facing page, in the equivalent 175–79, Horace goes about his quiet business of making us better by inducing reflection, posing two questions that make us ponder the worth of things. The first stresses succession, with death in the background:

> Sic, quia *perpetuus* nulli datur *usus,* & haeres
> Haeredem alterius, velut unda supervenit undam:
> Quid *vici* prosunt, aut *horrea*?
>
> (175–77)

> (So since to none perpetual use is given, and one heir
> succeeds the next as wave rolls down upon the wave before,
> what are estates or granaries worth?)

In rendering this, Pope begins with the striking contrast of a denunciatory peak from which he never descends very far into the Horatian lowlands of instruction:

> *Man?* and *for ever?* Wretch! What wou'dst thou have?
> Heir urges Heir, like Wave impelling Wave:
> All vast Possessions (just the same the case
> Whether you call them Villa, Park, or Chace)
> Alas, my Bathurst! what will they avail?
>
> (252–56)

He alters the wave metaphor—rendering "supervenit" (used with
both waves and heirs) by the forceful "urges" and "impelling"
makes succession more of a violent pushing aside. The "Whether
you call them" in 255 is a sarcastic direct address to the reader not
present in the Latin. "Alas" is a departure too; Horace has little
reason to say this, since he is merely describing a cyclic process:
heirs come and go. Pope, we shall soon see, envisions something
final, an end that involves good men, like Bathurst, as well as bad.
   Horace's second question brings death before us:

> quidve Calabris
> Saltibus adjecti Lucani; si metit Orcus
> Grandia cum parvis, non exorabilis auro?
>
> (177–79)

> (Why to Calabrian
> fields add new land in Lucania, if Orcus harvests
> great and small together and gold can't buy him off?)

This will provoke somber reflections, but they will not lack hope.
Although Horace shows us death, his theme is really life: since
death comes for rich and poor alike, therefore live well without
ambitions (and, Horace tells us later [207], without fear of death).
Living well is possible. Horace assumes a world which allows us
that. This becomes particularly clear when we see that Pope shares
neither this assumption nor, consequently, Horace's intention to
teach us how to live. He casts the Horatian question as an assertion
in order to deliver a final, crushing truth:

> Join *Cotswold* Hills to *Saperton's* fair Dale,
> Let rising Granaries and temples here,
> There mingled Farms and Pyramids appear,

Link Towns to Towns with Avenues of Oak,
Enclose whole Downs in Walls, 'tis all a joke!
Inexorable Death shall level all,
And Trees, and Stones, and Farms, and Farmer fall.

(257–63)

" 'Tis all a joke." Perhaps the linked towns and walled downs,
both unnatural in the discordant way of Timon's gardens in the
Epistle to Bathurst, signify a society in which city and country have
come awkwardly together (London let loose upon the countryside,
like London's noisy bards). At any rate, this society will not last.
Not even the stones and trees will last, let alone the farmer. Compared to this revelation, the similar scene at the end of Pope's
imitation of *Sat.* 2.2 seems almost to picture a natural decline. In
the later poem death descends on everything at once. Pope ignores
Horace's point that death is not "exorabilis auro," because he is no
longer talking about wealth and property and what they do to the
individual. He shows us the death of the world, and no one—not
even the admired Bathurst (256)—is able to escape. "And Trees,
and Stones, and Farms, and Farmer fall."

There then begins the Horatian ending of this imitation. With
Horace, Pope assumes a right to advise others how to think and
live, how to prepare for death. For both poets the theme is self-
acceptance, and each uses himself as an example. Horace is happy
to be "Extremi primorum, extremis usque priores" (204); "Behind
the foremost, and before the last" (303), says Pope, in quite faithful
translation. One can believe in the authenticity of this claim of
contentment when it comes from Horace, but not—after all the
imitation has shown previously, especially just previously—from
Pope. One can certainly believe that he has the right to give advice,
for his anger and sorrow testify to his concern, but the philosopher
who speaks as this poem ends has either failed to look at the world
the satirist has shown or has divorced himself from the passions the
satirist must feel.

Since un-Horatian passions burst from Pope upon an un-Horatian world, in which power is separated from intelligence and re-
sponsibility, why does he follow Horace at the poem's end, as well
as reinforcing earlier his own resemblance to Horace? In speculating, one may cite a tactical motive—Horace's good reputation,
which Pope would, as in the past, find worth borrowing. More
importantly, lines 157–79 of this imitation suggest that Pope likens
himself to Horace because he accepts, indeed fervently holds to,
Horace's definition of the ideal poet in the lines imitated, 109–25.

Certainly Pope "warms deeply to the idea that writing involves moral rigour and courage."[14] But beyond that, in describing the poet's duties and powers, *Epist.* 2.2 pictures an artist who fulfills himself by serving Rome. As we have seen, he must be a *censor* with words (110–14); in 122 the ideal poet "Luxuriantia compescet" ("cuts back wild growths"). The analogy with the Roman official implies that the poet should have a civil role. This, however, involves more than merely pruning the language. He keeps national tradition alive by "unearthing" ("eruet" [115]) words spoken by heroes of the Roman past: "vocabula rerum, / Quae priscis memorata Catonibus atque Cethegis" (116–17) ("the splendid names for things / once spoken by old Cato and Cethegus"). At the emotional climax of the passage, the poet is likened to a river or river god, enriching the land: "puroque simillimus amni, / *Fundet* opes, Latiumque beabit divite lingua" (120–21) ("like an unchoked stream, / the poet pours forth his wealth on Latium, a treasure of words").

Pope is no less serious, certainly. He declares that good poets will

> Pour the full Tide of Eloquence along,
> Serenely pure, and yet divinely strong,
> Rich with the Treasures of each foreign Tongue.
>
> (171–73)

Although not so "divinely strong" as the Horatian poet with his godlike, vitalizing "opes," those poets possess something of the divine who "In downright Charity revive the dead" (164)—dead words, of course. As in the source, these come out of a nation's history: "Words, that wise *Bacon,* or brave *Raleigh* spake" (168). True English poets should serve their country too.

However, while sharing with Horace this concept of what poets should do, Pope knows that he does not share with him the experience of living in a world in which leaders have reasonable standards and impose them on others. Reminding us of the difference, he shows how it affects him by creating in this passage an image of true poets as kings of language—an allusion not present in the source. They "Command old words" (167), rather than "unearth" them, and where Horace writes only "Adsciscet *nova:*" (119) ("enlists new words"), they "bid the new be *English,* Ages hence" (169). In the context of this poem, they are kings in opposition to the court (as well as to the false poet-kings of Merlin's Cave).

Certainly Pope is thinking of himself. Although he speaks of "poets," the passage closes (178–79) with a quotation from the

Essay on Criticism. In the suggested opposition of poet-king to court, one finds again the theme of the opposed orders present in the first two *Imitations* and in *Arbuthnot,* and in the poet's command over words there is a reflection of the supernatural power Pope uneasily confers on himself in his imitation of *Sat.* 2.2.

One can safely say that Pope accepts Horace's version of the ideal poet and would like to adapt it to his own situation. However, the entire poem warns against easily accepting the idea of the "genuine, withdrawn poet," of, that is, an Alexander Pope who remains "Alexander Pope still by staying away from Walpole's city and court."[15] First, the city appears to be coming after him in the form of its poets and its architecture. Second, the imitation rouses suspicions in readers concerning the morality of withdrawal. Finally, if Pope has decided to stay away, why does he return in satire, at least, to the court and to the toppling world it dominates?

One probable source of the anger and despair that become particularly visible in 212–63 is Pope's perception of the gap between himself as an opposition poet and Horace as a veteran member of Rome's ruling circle. This is the fully "Augustan" Horace, one remembers, who speaks and looks out from a very high place. From his retired country home, he sees not perfection, but at least a reasonable arrangement into which he fits. For him there is one order, not two, and he speaks for those in power; indeed, at this stage in his career, one is prone to identify him with those in power.

For Pope, to be genuine means opposing power, which true poetry blasts. This may do some good; it is certainly laudable as the response of a patriotic poet to national decline, presided over by a worthless king, court, judiciary, Parliament, and so on. Of all those who have responsibilities to the nation, only the poet does his job and only, it seems, by opposing everyone else. But, gazing upon Horace, Pope may be expected to show the strain of going it alone.

The Imitator of Horace has never taken a simple view of the question that precedes application: how is his world like my own? To this, all the *Imitations* discussed so far are answers that take the form of involving, disturbing poetry in which issues are raised, but not resolved. This irresolution affects our experience of reading the poems, but does not make them inferior: it reveals a concerned, probing, and interesting mind, rather than Pope's failure to be clear about things easily understood.

The Second Epistle of the Second Book of Horace, Imitated, in the writing of which Pope confronted the fully "Augustan" Horace of *Epist.* 2.2, does not settle the problems that arise out of the relationship he sees and resees, makes and remakes, between

Rome and England and between Horace and himself; if anything, it complicates them. Perhaps Pope then felt compelled to work toward definite answers, no matter how unpalatable. At any rate, a degree of certainty seems to descend upon him in the next of the *Imitations*, the *Epistle to Augustus*, resulting in a clearer but surely no less complex vision.

8

Confronting the Age

The First Epistle of the Second Book of Horace, Imitated

Pope's next Horatian imitation, based on *Epist.* 2.1, is the *Epistle to Augustus,* written in 1737. This, the most famous of all the *Imitations,* has received from Howard D. Weinbrot what he himself described as a "frankly revisionist interpretation." One more quotation will serve to sum up his case: "What Pope wishes us to see [in this imitation] is not that George Augustus is unlike but shockingly like his Roman namesake": like him, that is, as a suppressor of freedom.[1] But although the poem shows at several points that Pope certainly preferred a state of *"Free People"* to an *"Absolute Empire,"* as his Advertisement (from which I quote) makes clear, he just as certainly did not accept a one-dimensional view of Augustus as a tyrant. Few people did. In chapter 2, it has been demonstrated that neither period nor politics can be counted on to make a dogmatic anti-Augustan out of Pope.

Even if he had been that, comparison with Augustus would still have been an improbable weapon with which to attack George, for, as chapter 2 also explains, the age perceived great differences between them. Augustus was thought to have usurped power, although the Republic's collapse made such an action, by someone, inevitable, but even the opposition considered George the rightful king. In addition, Augustus had obviously great personal and intellectual gifts, which he could use for ill as well as good, but George was known for his dullness and pliability.

Finally, Horace's *Epist.* 2.1 is a most unlikely vehicle to choose for attacking the king by implying his similarity to the emperor. Horace's Augustus, whom readers of the imitation will often have in view, is a leader in whom the norms of political leadership and enlightened literary patronage vitally coincide. Although every reader of Horace's poem may perceive this figure a little differently, unless something in the imitation compels, a reader should not discard the fundamental Horatian image for a tyrannical Augustus extrinsic to the Latin poem. In my opinion, no one has shown that anything in the imitation does so compel.[2]

If I am correct, the traditional interpretation is the right one, after all. The king is *unlike* his "Roman namesake." Pope employs Horace's Augustus as an example of a monarch who uses power wisely, and by means of this good example he judges George.[3] At the same time he evaluates the power of Dulness that is immanent in George and George's age, while examining the consequences of this power for the world and himself.

These consequences are alarming, to say the least. And yet, despite them, Pope often sounds like Horace. With Erskine-Hill, I am impressed by his ability to "blend a friendly, confident and intelligent manner—one appropriate to an Augustan Age in the positive sense of that term—with the sense of a political and cultural crisis."[4] The imitation of *Epist*. 2.2, in contrast, responds to crisis, Pope's own and his culture's, with evident rage and despair. In the *Epistle to Augustus,* of course, Pope relies much more on irony than in the earlier imitation, but this does not indicate that he is less angry or less despairing. The presence of irony suggests, in fact, his surer knowledge of how little he can do about the people and forces he fears and hates.

Epist. 2.1 affords Pope ample opportunity to consider the major differences between Horace's world and career and his own. By offering a complex but overwhelmingly favorable portrait of Augustus, it leads him, for the first time in the *Imitations,* to focus on George II and on what he means to England. Moreover, because the epistle elucidates more fully than any other *sermo* the value of poetry that supports entrenched power, Pope must examine with particular thoroughness the meaning of his role as a poet of the opposition. In previous *Imitations* he had also considered his plight as a patriot-poet (or opposition poet-king) who must work against a corrupt center of power, but in choosing *Epist*. 2.1 to imitate, he opposed this role to Horace's noblest description of the poet working *for* power. The result of these applications, as shall be explained, is a deeper sense of the futility of being a poet, even a poet who is a virtuous satirist.

Pope's imitation follows the structure of the Latin poem, in which it is appropriate to distinguish five parts: lines 1–17, 18–92, 93–138, 139–213, and 214–70.[5] The equivalent sections in the English *Epistle to Augustus* are 1–30, 31–138, 139–240, 241–347, and 348–419. While the first and last sections of *Epist*. 2.1 contain much explicit praise of Augustus, Pope's 1–30 and 348–419 contain much ironic praise of George, and we can detect the irony without needing to refer to Horace. Overblown or bathetic language gives the game away, as in these two couplets from beginning and end respectively:

> Wonder of Kings! like whom, to mortal eyes
> None e'er has risen, and none e'er shall rise.
>
> (29–30)

> Oh! could I mount on the Maeonian wing,
> Your Arms, your Actions, your Repose to sing!
>
> (394–95)

However, Horace's Augustus yet matters. For of him it can be truly said, "*Nil oriturum* alias, *nil ortum tale* fatentes" (17) ("we admit that none has been, nor will become, your like"); and, if Horace chose "*res* componere *gestas*" (251) ("to write an epic"), he could sing about truly grand exploits, both in the field and at home.[6] Thus the norm of Augustus deepens and validates the evident irony Pope directs at George.

But the irony in the *Epistle to Augustus* is not always so accessible, and detecting it may largely depend on comparing imitation to source. Irony of the most crushing and wintry kind, unnoticed by critics of the poem, occurs at the close (229–40) of the third or central section, undermining what seems to be honest praise for an honest rural choir. Since the Latin lines imitated, 132–38, form the climax of *Epist.* 2.1, the equivalent English passage significantly affects the meaning of Pope's entire poem. To understand it, one must not only compare the English lines to the Latin, but also consider the analogous placement of each passage within its poem. For this purpose, nothing need be added to my brief comparison of Pope's and Horace's first and fifth sections. Let us turn then to the second and fourth sections, beginning with the Latin epistle.

The second section, 18–92, departs smoothly from the first's closing observation that Augustus differs from other heroes in being widely revered in his own time. Unfortunately, Horace now asserts, the Roman public fails to apply the same good judgment to literature. Prejudiced by senseless veneration for age, both critics and common people rate the older Latin poets too high, Horace's generation too low. The truth is that the earlier poets were often lazy and careless. In the midst of this attack on them, Horace pauses to admit that, for all their faults, he would not like to see their work destroyed (69–71).[7] This concession may signal his awareness that he is overstating his case against the poets, when his real enemy is popular bias.

In the fourth section (139–213), Horace continues to criticize the contemporary public, attacking theater audiences for being noisy and for preferring spectacle to words. Here, however, he takes a more balanced view of the early literature. Rude and rustic in its origins (in Fescennine verse [145]), it was rescued by Roman moral strictness: imposed upon the poets, this restrained their violent wit (152–55). Moreover, the poets fell under the influence of Greece, as Rome grew into empire: "Graecia capta, ferum victorem cepit, & Artes / Intulit agresti Latio" (156–57) ("Greece taken took her fierce captor captive and bore / her arts to Latium's farms"). After the Punic Wars were over, and there was leisure to consider and emulate Greek literature (161–63), Roman poets did particularly well with tragedy, an appropriate genre for men "natura sublimis, & acer" (165) (of a "nature" with its own "nobility and force").

Abruptly leaving the past for the Augustan present, Horace finds that this bold and lofty spirit still survives. For line 166 employs the present tense: "Nam spirat tragicum satis, & feliciter audet" ("we have true tragic spirit and the gift of daring well"). In addition, although Horace does not mention them at this exact point, clearly Greek rules and models also survive. So, unfortunately, do the vestiges of the crude Roman poetic style of the past (159–60). And two further obstacles stand in the way of literary excellence: the public's bad taste and the "sublimis" but impatient Roman poet's scorn of revision (167). However, Greece's art and Rome's native spirit obviously complement one another, and the contemporary Roman poet has the opportunity to combine these two heritages in his work. To assure readers of this, in section three Horace has already shown the promise of their union fulfilled in great poetry.

But what does Pope make of Horace's second and fourth sections? Both his 31–138 and 241–347, which are *not* predominantly ironic, make statements roughly similar to those in *Epist.* 2.1. The people are said to look down on the moderns, to favor the older English writers (31–42), who had both "greater faults than we," and—as Pope goes beyond his model to accommodate the truth as he saw it—"greater Virtues" (95–96). Following Horace, Pope complains about English theater audiences (304–37) and also observes that Otway, Shakespeare, and Dryden (these specific poets taking the place of the Roman poet "natura sublimis") were deficient in polishing and revising (278–81). But Dryden was, at least, "copious" (280), while the "Tragic spirit was our own, / And full in Shakespear, fair in Otway shone" (276–77). Finally, France, in the place of Greece, imparted "correctness" (272), along with the models of Racine and Corneille (274).

Pope seems to look with less confidence than does Horace on the possibility of foreign art and native spirit merging. First, he offers no equivalent for the present tense "spirat tragicum"; the "Tragic spirit . . . shone," not shines. Further comparison with Horace subtly diminishes the importance of "correctness," which arrived "Late, very late" (272), not simply "Serus" (161), in an England "tir'd" after "civil war" (273), rather than at peace after defeating an external enemy: "post *Punica bella* quietus" (162) ("after our Punic victories gave us peace"). But Pope's was not, of course, an age of tragedy, and the rules surely had a greater influence after 1660 than before. Rather than overlook the differences between England and Rome, Pope admits them and thus makes his historical survey more accurate. Despite the differences, the literary inheritance he describes is essentially similar to Horace's Roman legacy.

For Horace, Greek rules and models represent a larger whole, and so do Roman moral strictness and nobility of soul. One recognizes this because in the epistle's third or central section, lines 93–138, the Greek inheritance becomes identified with art, the Roman intrinsic moral sense with virtue. Making the adjustments necessary for imitation, Pope sets up a similar opposition of qualities. However, comparing Horace's central section to his, lines 139–240, one sees that while Augustan Rome achieved a union of art and virtue, George's England does not. The consequences go beyond literature.

At the beginning, Pope follows Horace, whose comparison of fifth-century Greece to primitive Rome seems, oddly enough, to caricature both cultures (93–107). His Greeks are a race of gifted but trifling children, always ready to drop one artistic craze and rush on to the next, while the early-rising Romans know only hard work and clean living. As Fraenkel points out, Horace has chosen to ignore everything in Greece's greatest age but artistic inventiveness, everything in old Rome but moral gravity.[8] In the imitation's opposition of cultures in the parallel lines 139–68, fifth-century Greece becomes the Restoration, shown here as essentially alien: "In every Taste of foreign Courts improv'd" (141). It also boiled with talent and with too many enthusiasms. For early Rome Pope supplies a vaguely defined early English period, frugal and pious (161–68).

In describing the Restoration, the imitation makes some suggestive departures from the Latin. A period fertile in the arts, it corrupted them with the immorality that shamed its court (151–54), a quality not explicitly present in Horace's portrait of the Greeks. Moreover, Pope extends Greek cultural fickleness to English politics: "But Britain, changeful as a Child at play, / Now calls in Princes, and now turns away" (155–56). Both political instability and moral corruption, however, can be easily inferred from Horace's sketch of a mercurial Greece. As for the "sober Englishman" (161) and his family, Pope has based them squarely on Horace's sober old Romans.

Immediately following the initial exaggerated contrast in the epistle, Horace pictures a contemporary Rome that seems to have become Greek in the childish way he has just described. Their native seriousness apparently outgrown, the people are "levis" now (108), the city filled with would-be poets in the grip of "*Scribendi studio*" (109). When Pope leaps ahead to his own time, he illustrates in a similar way the effects of the "Poetick Itch" (169). At this point, however, he does begin to differ sharply from Horace.

Let us return to the Latin epistle a few lines beyond "*Scribendi studio.*"[9] At line 118 Horace turns from the talentless mob to the true poet. They will inevitably move on to some new craze, but he "versus amat, hoc studet unum" (120) ("he loves poetry, his only passion"). Such deep involvement leaves him uninterested in money or in cheating anyone to get it (122–23), but it also unfits him for taking seriously any ordinary emergency (121) or for fighting in a war (124). It is remarkable, then, how quickly Horace transforms this peculiar citizen into a worthy public man, *"utilis urbi"* (124) ("of social use"). There is little or no irony in the picture of the poet drawn in 126–31:

> Os tenerum pueri balbumque poeta figurat:
> Torquet ab *obscaenis* iam nunc sermonibus aurem;
> Mox etiam pectus praeceptis format amicis,
> *Asperitatis, & invidiae corrector, & irae.*
> Recte facta refert; orientia tempora notis
> Instruit exemplis: *inopem* solatur, & *aegrum.*

(The poet trains the child's blurred and stammering speech,
teaches him to turn his ear away from harmful talk,
and soon with friendly words begins to shape his mind,
as the corrector of fierceness and envy and wrath.
He describes fine deeds and instructs with great examples
each successive year, he gives the sick and hopeless comfort.)[10]

This poet's purposes are deeply moral, and his success at carrying them out assures us that he has talent and proceeds with art.

Sounding the first note of the theme that will triumphantly conclude this section, Horace shows the Greek and Roman legacies
merging in the contemporary Augustan poet.

How did this introverted versifier ever happen to enter the world
and take on a public role? Since his own nature would hardly have
prompted him, the world must have summoned him forth; in the
context of this particular epistle, it seems clear that the world did so
through Augustus. Patron of good poets and architect of a unified
Rome fit to inspire even the epic muse, the emperor had, moreover,
specifically called for the writing of the *Aeneid,* to which 130–31
probably refer; of Horace's *Carmen Saeculare,* the subject of 132–
38; and of this very *Epistle to Augustus.*[11] He has brought the poet
in, made him *"utilis urbi."*

The imitation's lines 189–200, following Horace's 119–25, also
picture the poet as detached from what are supposed to be ordinary
activities. These, however, are probably more criminal and certainly
more violent than their Latin counterparts. After noting that
"rarely Av'rice taints the tuneful mind" (192), Pope remarks that
the poet "ne'er rebels, or plots, like other men," and that "Flight of
Cashiers [involved in the South Sea Bubble], or Mobs, he'll never
mind" (194–95). Having echoed and amplified his earlier allusion to
a restive Britain, Pope builds upon this suspect ground the passage
meant to prove the poet "(tho' no Soldier) useful to the State"
(204).

Following Horace, Pope praises poets as teachers of the language
(205–8), hinting perhaps at "the inability of the new German Kings
of England to speak English."[12] At this point, he begins a drastic
departure from the Latin text. First he condemns the "worthless
thing" who stoops to "praise some monster of a King" and "please
a lewd, or un-believing Court" (209–12). We think of George II, of
laureate Cibber, of George's corrupt minister and court. Although
the imitation then refers to earlier kings and poets, the first impression persists. So does the animosity toward courts persist: Pope
admires Roscommon's "unspotted Bays" in "Charles's days" and
regrets the "Courtly stains" of Addison (213–15). Swift, of course,
receives the highest praise, not merely for avoiding spot or stain,
but for combating the predatory court of George I: "The Rights of
Court attack'd, a Poet sav'd" (224).

To be *"utilis urbi,"* it appears, the poet must not cooperate with
those in power; to be most virtuous, he must actually oppose them.
Like the Augustan poetry of Horace's lines 126–31, the literature
such opposition produces is unquestionably virtuous; it can be
artistic, obviously, if written with art. However, while comparing

imitation to original establishes these likenesses, it suggests as well an obvious but fundamental difference. The Augustan poetry of Vergil and Horace sprang from the poets' respect for power sanctioned, they believed, through significant achievements and from their gratitude for generous, informed patronage. In England, Pope leads us to see, no such power and patronage exist. One's awareness of the contrast injects a note of futility into Swift's noble triumph.

Moreover, in considering the gap between poetry supporting power and poetry that opposes it, one finds the following unhappy implication. Since the virtuous poet must avoid and should oppose courts and kings, he will be of necessity discouraged from working in the genres they traditionally encourage and support. So epic goes to Blackmore, who gives us *Prince Arthur,* and patriotic lyric, like Horace's Roman odes, to Cibber. Even the modest Horatian *sermo,* one virtuous English poet may uneasily recall, assumes the existence of values shared between poet and court. Thus poetic achievement is unfortunately limited. To say nothing of less literary modes of attack such as the political pamphlet, satire can never devote more than a fraction of its considerable energies to picturing the desirable case, the ideally normative in culture or politics, against which the undesirable is measured. It can make us see what is wrong more easily than what is right.

Pope's conception of a virtuous literature appropriate for his age leaves no room for the creation of shared visions—Vergil's, for example—that can bring and keep a people together. Then, at the very center of his poem, in the twelve lines directly following the passage on Swift, Pope pictures metaphorically the results of England's failure to achieve, on this lofty level, a grand synthesis of art and virtue. Contrast with the source greatly contributes to the meaning, since Horace gives us exactly this synthesis in the parallel lines, 132–38, the "crown of his epistle."[13]

Though he well might have, he does not refer to Vergil here. Instead, he sheds his usual modesty to focus on his own triumph, not in any *sermo,* nor even in the Roman Odes, but in the remarkable achievement of the *Carmen Saeculare.* It has always been understood that Horace is describing the performance of his own choral hymn:

> Castis cum pueris ignara puella mariti
> Disceret unde *preces,* vatem ni Musa dedisset?
> Poscit opem Chorus, & *praesentia numina* sentit;
> Caelestes implorat aquas docta prece blandus;
> Avertit morbos, *metuenda pericula* pellit;

Impetrat & *Pacem,* & locupletem frugibus annum:
Carmina Di superi placantur, carmine Manes.

(How would the chaste boys and the innocent, unwed girl
have learned the prayers without a poet given by the Muse?
The chorus asks for help and feels the gods' response,
asks heaven for rain and pleases, taught how to pray;
it prevents disease, makes dreadful perils keep far off;
it brings us peaceful times and a season of rich crops.
The sacred song delights the gods above and those below.)

The emotional power of this passage reflects its structural importance within the poem. Although Horace has already shown Roman
virtue and Greek art combined in Augustan poetry, here is the
fullest expression of the power of poetry to "combine the moral and
political virtues of a Roman with the best gifts of the Greek
Muse."[14] Little wonder that the gods approve.

Does Pope claim anything at all like this for contemporary literature in the equivalent lines of the imitation, 229–40? Obviously he
does not follow Horace in claiming it for something of his own, such
as his satires or perhaps the *Essay on Man,* in which both art and
virtue are obviously present. Instead, the *Epistle to Augustus* trans-
ports us, not to Twickenham and the poet at work, but to "country
pews" where we get a chorus for a chorus, at least, as well as what
appears to be similar divine support. "Heav'n," after all, "is won":

Not but there are, who merit other palms;
Hopkins and Sternhold glad the heart with Psalms;
The Boys and Girls whom Charity maintains,
Implore your help in these pathetic strains:
How could Devotion touch the country pews,
Unless the Gods bestow'd a proper Muse?
Verse chears their leisure, Verse assists their work,
Verse prays for Peace, or sings down Pope and Turk.
The silenc'd Preacher yields to potent strain,
And feels that grace his pray'r besought in vain,
The blessing thrills thro' all the lab'ring throng,
And Heav'n is won by violence of Song.

However, few would claim much art for the Psalms as translated
by Hopkins and Sternhold. Pope himself in a letter to Swift, called
them both "bad poets." The same letter, moreover, hatched the pun
in line 236: "sings down Pope and Turk."[15] Since we know that
Pope is virtuous, this hints that something in or about the song is
vicious. In that case, it is meant to oppose the *Carmen Saeculare* in
both its aesthetic and moral qualities.

This, in fact, it does, as study of the passage will show, for, while the quality of the translation insures that these Psalms lack art, the chorus's performance deprives them of virtue as well. Through Pope's metaphors and expressive language, the chorus becomes a destructive army that "sings down" a "silenc'd [not silent] Preacher," as well as Pope and Turk. In the delivery, "pathetic strains" turn into a "potent strain," and the "lab'ring throng" plods ahead until "Heav'n is won by violence of Song." Horace's singers seek help and please the gods; the English "Boys and Girls" attack Pope (or poetry), the preacher (rightful authority), and heaven (the source of order).

Associated with this strange spiritual violence is the striking gap between the two choruses in the matter of location. On the day of its performance, the *Carmen Saeculare* held the center of the Roman world. Horace wrote it for the Secular Games ordered by Augustus, a massive public celebration of the kind that occupies the consciousness of an entire people. No wonder, then, that Horace's hymn draws all the world evenly about it, reaching out with equal success to both the gods above and those below. In contrast, these Psalms are wailed or roared in far-off "country pews." The low status of the singers (high-born youths made up the Roman chorus) and, somewhat indirectly, the distant composition date (1562) of the Hopkins-Sternhold translation further suggest the peripheral nature of the performance. Radical displacement from the center of things correlates with the perversion of sacred song.

This state of affairs is the more lamentable because England has a tradition similar to Rome's: one legacy of foreign art, another of native virtue. But their complete fusion occurs only in satire of the court. While the performance of the *Carmen Saeculare* in *Epist* 2.1 represents the vital coherence of Rome, in the imitation sacred song thrust out to the kingdom's furthest edge becomes a sign of gathering chaos.

Like the poets besieging Twickenham in *Arbuthnot,* Pope's singers intend no harm. They too are merely the instruments of the Goddess, of Dulness. Her chief instrument, however, is the king. This becomes clear by contrast with what Augustus is responsible for in Rome: the Latin epistle's first and fifth sections inform us that he supports both Rome's peace and Rome's poetry, and the third presents as an ideal poem a work he had asked to be written for his festival by his poet. The *Carmen Saeculare* issued from the top and center of the state; from there, in Pope's traditional conception, order should originate. But George, compared to Augustus, is a human vacuum. No order can emanate from him. Instead, says

Pope, addressing his ruler, "when you nodded, o'er the land and deep, / Peace stole her wing, and wrapt the world in sleep" (400–401). Dulness has the king, and so is free to take the chorus and perhaps, except for Pope, all poetry.

Against such a force, why should he carry on with satire? This is a reasonable, if painful, question for him to raise in this imitation, and Horace's "recusatio" in 250–59, his refusal to write, would allow Pope to raise it in a fairly straightforward way; but he lets this particular opportunity pass. Horace firmly but politely declines to compose heroic poems, although he knows that the emperor's actions indeed deserve them.[16] He employs tact, Pope irony: "Oh! could I mount on the Maeonian wing." But since, of course, Pope is given no heroic deeds to sing about and has no requests from George to sing, he is not really declining anything here. However, the *Epistle to Augustus* may still contain a sincere element of "recusatio." At least it suggests not only that satire is of little use, but also, that Pope may cease to write it.

"But Verse alas! your Majesty disdains" (404). Satire is powerless, as ever, to affect George. By exposing the power of Dulness as she works through him, the imitation raises once again the question of what good any satire can do. In considering this in earlier *Imitations,* Pope is sometimes visibly angry or despairing; in the *Augustus* he keeps his temper. The irony is marvelous, but its very moderation signals Pope's sense of a distance between poet and king, between poet and nation, so great it makes strong feeling pointless. That would make satire pointless too.

Moreover, the very last lines of the *Epistle to Augustus* suggest, through differences from the equivalent Latin passage, that Pope is seriously considering the advice Fortescue gave him at the beginning of his career as Horace's imitator: "I'd write no more." First Pope implies, with nothing similar in his source, that the ironic satire occupying much of the *Augustus* might get him into trouble: "Besides, a fate attends on all I write, / That when I aim at praise, they say I bite" (408–9). Then he attacks "vile Encomium" and vows that he will never flatter:

> A vile Encomium doubly ridicules;
> There's nothing blackens like the ink of fools;
> If true, a woful likeness, and if lyes,
> "Praise undeserv'd is scandal in disguise:"
> Well may he blush, who gives it, or receives;
> And when I flatter, let my dirty leaves
> (Like Journals, Odes, and such forgotten things
> As Eusden, Philips, Settle, writ of Kings)

Cloath Spice, line trunks, or flutt'ring in a row,
Befringe the rails of Bedlam and Sohoe.

(410–19)

Surely there is no irony intended in these lines; of course Pope
will not write flattery. Comparison with the source will indicate,
however, that here Pope is, in addition, considering the prospect of
not writing satire. For Horace deals with the topic of flattery in a
very different way:

Nil moror officium quod me gravat; ac neque *ficto*
In pejus voltu proponi cereus usquam,
Nec prave factis decorari versibus, opto:
Ne rubeam *pingui* donatus *munere;* & una
Cum scriptore meo, capsa porrectus aperta,
Deferar in vicum vendentem thus & odores,
Et piper, & quicquid chartis amicitur ineptis.

(264–70)

(I don't like graceless honors for myself, a wax bust
set up somewhere that makes me uglier than I am,
or a sloppy, awkward poem in which I'm glorified.
That idiotic gift would make me blush and insure
my passage in a box, a kind of coffin, with my poet,
to the market where people sell incense and perfume
and pepper, and anything wrapped up in wasted paper.)

Rather than swear never to flatter, Horace expresses disdain for
those who flatter *him*. Obviously there is in this a message for
Augustus, who should also reject the praise of flatterers; Horace
implies a parallel between the emperor, the ruler of Rome, and
himself, the ruler of wit.

A notable gap, then, exists between imitation and source, for
"who gives it, or receives" barely glances at the theme of the poet
flattered as if he were a monarch. However, *Arbuthnot* tells us how
Pope is pestered by particularly stupid flatterers, as well as besieged at Twickenham by hordes of suppliants; and various *Imitations* show him ruling both this "counterkingdom" and the entire
province of poetry. Kings are flattered, as Horace warns Augustus.
Poetry makes Pope a king—because of the kind of poetry he writes,
a king in opposition. When he ignores an opportunity to scorn his
flatterers, he suggests that he may abdicate.

"I'd write no more," said Fortescue. For all its chatty urbanity, its
Horatian style, the *Epistle to Augustus* makes an impressive case
for silence.

9

Toward Silence

Of course Pope did not cease to write after the *Augustus*. His imitations of *Epist.* 1.6 and 1.1 appeared in 1738, along with some minor exercises in the same genre, and the *Epilogue to the Satires*. A few years later came that marvel of creative energy, *The New Dunciad*. But all these poems, including the exultantly destructive *Dunciad*, show him turning, in some way, toward a final silence. Among the causes for the late development of this theme in his career should be reckoned his application of what he found in Horace, for this led him to measure his own age by Augustan standards. Thus, he became particularly aware of its social incoherence under dull George, compared to the order of Augustan Rome, and of his own isolation, compared to Horace's sense of being at the center of things.

The Sixth Epistle of the First Book of Horace Imitated

But it must be explained how the imitation of *Epist.* 1.6 shows Pope coming detectably closer to accepting the counsel of Fortescue, since the poem does incorporate a vein of potent political satire. This becomes most conspicuous when it has no equivalent in the Latin—as in lines 13–17 and 83–84. It is perhaps strongest when Pope turns Horace's general point, made through a reference to the *Odyssey*—that immorality unfits one to be a citizen (61–64)—into an attack directed specifically at the court. Chartres, K[innoul]l, and Ty[rawle]y were connected with Walpole, as John Aden points out,[1] and Pope does not hesitate to include the king among his targets:

> Or shall we ev'ry Decency confound,
> Thro' Taverns, Stews, and Bagnio's take our round,
> Go dine with Chartres, in each Vice out-do
> K——l's lewd Cargo, or Ty——y's Crew,

From Latian Syrens, French Circaean Feasts,
Return well travell'd, and transform'd to Beasts,
Or for a Titled Punk, or Foreign Flame,
Renounce our Country, and degrade our Name?

(118–25)

Moreover, he urges William Murray, the poem's addressee, to interest himself in politics and take action against the court. He makes this course attractive to Murray (and, certainly, to other readers) by extending the prospect of interment in Westminster Abbey, "Where Murray (long enough his Country's pride) / Shall be no more than Tully, or than Hyde!" (52–53). At this point Horace, referring to the long dead Numa and Ancus, wants only to remind us of the inevitability of death (25–27).[2]

We might, however, consider that in none of the preceding *Imitations of Horace* has Pope seriously urged anyone to act. He has been the principal actor, both as the protector of other potential combatants (or weary refugees) involved in the war against the court and Dulness, and as a satirist, foremost in the field. But he has fought on in this way burdened by the suspicion that his enemies' stupidity armors them against his satire, which in the imitation of *Epist.* 1.6 becomes secondary to and essentially part of the exhortation to Murray. It is almost shocking to see Pope reduced to a mere adviser. This role is obviously virtuous, but his assuming of it implies his belief that the satirist matters less than an untested man of action.

Thus Pope turns toward silence, at least in his customary persona as attacking satirist. Moreover, at the end of this imitation, he considers the possibility that as an adviser he might as well be silent too: Murray may not take his advice. This prospect emerges in his final four lines, which, although they seem to one critic part of a "concluding affirmation," strike me—contrasting them to the equivalent Latin 65–66—as a confession of futility even grimmer than the "utter uncertainty" glimpsed by another.[3]

Perhaps it should be made clear that contrasts with Horace matter. Although J. W. Tupper, seconded by Aden, judges that Pope " 'gives a serious tone to Horace's flippancy,' " *Epist.* 1.6 probably contains less flippancy than any other *sermo*. W. Y. Sellar calls it "the most elaborate, the most enigmatical, and the most impersonal of all the ethical Epistles."[4] Pope is serious, but so is Horace. His advice in the first line, *"Nil Admirari"* ("Never be astonished"), refers to the balanced spiritual condition the ancients

prized as the goal of philosophy and knew as *ataraxia* or *apatheia.*
It is rare for Horace to present his teachings so directly, so uncon-
versationally, rare for him to ascend to the solemnity of "Hunc
Solem, & Stellas, & decedentia certis / Tempora momentis" (3–4)
("The sun in the sky, the stars, the constant motion / of the sea-
sons") or the denunciatory power of "Cui *potior patria* fuit inter-
dicta voluptas" (64) ("To whom their country mattered less than did
forbidden joy").

Pope borrows strength from Horace by imitating a particularly
serious *sermo,* altering the message in order to counsel the cultiva-
tion of virtue for action's sake; Horace proposes the same course,
but for the individual's sake. At one point Pope may appear to think
that virtue can be had rather easily. Referring to moral ills as "the
Mind's Disease," he comments, "There, all Men may be cur'd,
whene'er they please" (58–59). But the lines immediately preceding,
as will soon be seen, show that men generally do not make wise
choices. Moreover, most men do not equal Cornbury, who immediately proves to be the standard: "Would ye be blest? despise low
Joys, low Gains; / Disdain whatever Cornbury disdains" (60–61).
The tenor of the entire poem, until the very end, shows that Murray
is being called upon to make a difficult effort, to rise far above the
human average.

This is, of course, distressingly low, as Pope makes clear in a
striking departure from Horace's 28–29: "Si latus, aut renes morbo
tententur acuto, / Qu[a]ere fugam morbi—" ("If disease attacks
your chest or kidneys, get medicine / to drive it out"). This is a
given on which to help build an argument for moral health: take
similar action against moral disorders, such as greed. But Pope,
dwelling on physical illness, extends it to all humanity and makes of
it a sign of reason perverted by self-destructive men who, in their
last extremities, resort to quacks like Joshua Ward and Thomas
Dover:

> Rack'd with Sciatics, martyr'd with the Stone,
> Will any mortal let himself alone?
> See Ward by batter'd Beaus invited over,
> And des'prate Misery lays hold on Dover.
>
> (54–57)

Obviously the world needs reforming, and, if not Murray alone,
perhaps a generation of Murrays might be equal to the task. However, the Horatian source compels Pope to consider the possibility
that Murray may decline the exhortation to become his "Country's

pride." In the Latin epistle's conclusion, probably its least formal passage in tone, Horace first sneers at the hedonistic doctrines of the Greek poet Mimnermus, then blithely considers the prospect that the reader will not accept Horace's own teachings:

> Si (Mimnermus uti censet) sine *amore, jocisque,*
> Nil es jucundum; vivas in amore, jocisque.
>   Vive, vale! si quid novisti rectius istis,
> Candidus imperti: si non, his utere mecum.
>
> (65–68)

> (If, as Mimnermus likes to think, without love and games
> nothing can give pleasure, spend your life in love and games.
> Well, good luck. If you have advice more helpful than mine,
> be open and share it. If not, use mine along with me.)

Pope renders the first two of the four lines just quoted in his 126–29:

> If, after all, we must with Wilmot own,
> The Cordial Drop of Life is Love alone,
> And Swift cry wisely, "Vive la Bagatelle!"
> The Man that loves and laughs, must sure do well.

This is less cheerful than it sounds. Since the immediately preceding lines 118–25, quoted earlier, focus disapprovingly on sexual excesses, Rochester is a decidedly suspect exemplar. Nor does his poem, "A Letter from Artemisia in the Town to Chloe in the Country," from which Pope takes "Cordial Drop," show much confidence in love: Artemisia calls it "that cordial drop heaven in our cup has thrown," but this description comes within a context of complaint about how "this lewd town" has corrupted love, now "grown, like play, to be an arrant trade."[5] As for Swift here, although " 'Vive la Bagatelle' " was indeed his "rule" (Butt, p. 246), he appears in the *Epistle to Augustus* as the exemplary poet-patriot. His conduct in this role should guide Murray's public conduct, Pope must believe, not his rule for private life. After the satire in this poem, the "Man that loves and laughs" exemplifies only weary cynicism.

Pope then concludes on a casual note apparently quite close to that of the source's "Vive, vale!":

> Adieu—if this advice appear the worst,
> E'en take the Counsel which I gave you first:

> Or better Precepts if you can impart,
> Why do, I'll follow them with all my heart.

(130–33)

But since each poem offers a different initial "Counsel"—"*Nil Admirari*" for your own sake, " 'Not to Admire' " for your country's—the meanings of the conclusions sharply differ. Horace can gaze with equanimity upon the prospect of failing to convince a single friend, not in this case Augustus or Maecenas or another great man. (His addressee, Numicius, is unknown.) By his own air of unconcern, in fact, he actually illustrates the efficaciousness of "*Nil Admirari.*" In contrast, Pope cannot afford to accept with a smile the possibility of *his* reader not taking "the Counsel which I gave you first," and so the smile that appears is false.

Further proof comes from the fact that, as Bogel notes, in its last couplet the imitation reverses the Latin epistle's sequence of ideas. Horace concludes by recommending once again his own counsel: ". . . use mine along with me," while Pope, after asking for "better Precepts," concludes, "I'll follow them with all my heart." He has, we know, shown how vital is the action for which he has called. Rather than a cordial expression of boundless confidence in the judgment of a young, untested man, or even a generation of such men, this reversal indicates either "utter uncertainty," in Bogel's reading, along with a "bleak perception of the relativity of . . . rules, precepts, and paradigms,"[6] or something perhaps even more depressing: an admission by Pope that, although he believes in the value of certain rules and precepts, there may be no point in fighting for them.

The latter interpretation seems more probable to me. All Pope's poetry, including this imitation, affirms the value of certain standards. His fear is that others do not recognize or respect them, not that they are only relative. Even a temporary conversion to relativism seems unlikely. Pope knows what kind of world he lives in, for he has judged it by those standards, some of which he shares with Horace. Once so ready to carry on the war against the powers that corrupt, he now implicitly declines battle and even looks with resignation upon the possibility that it may not matter whether Murray listens to him or not.[7]

The First Epistle of the First Book of Horace Imitated

The last of the *Imitations of Horace* attacks the court, but without urging any action upon Bolingbroke, the addressee. This does not mean, however, the poet's rededication to satire, despite the quantity of political satire in the poem. After considering the question of satire's effect upon both its victims and the satirist, who must be agitated to write it, Pope chooses to withdraw from the corrupt world that provokes it. He inclines us to admire his spirit, rather than to feel sorry for him, partly because of the triumphs of this imitation: strength in denouncing vice, genuineness in invoking the ideals of philosophy and friendship. It is nonetheless a confession of defeat.

My view will surprise recent critics who consider this a strongly political poem, a virtual opposition manifesto from a "fully committed" Pope. But the political element has probably been overemphasized. Howard Erskine-Hill, aware that the imitation of *Epist.* 1.1 "has often been cited as showing a bolder and deeper hostility to court and government than [Pope] had yet expressed," warns that this hostility "is far from the whole truth that balanced literary criticism must acknowledge."[8] In my reading, this last of the *Imitations of Horace* contains a dialogue between social concerns, which call Pope toward satire, and personal needs, which lead him to philosophy. The latter win, and Pope retreats for his soul's sake, counseling the same course to Bolingbroke.

To understand this, one must consider the model poem. *Epist.* 1.1 may be divided into four sections: 1–27, 28–66, 67–90, 91–105. (Pope's Latin text, to which these numbers refer, omits the lines conventionally numbered 49–51.) The first part contains the most concrete element of *recusatio:* addressing Maecenas, Horace rejects his old patron's request for lyric poetry, protesting that the time has come for the poet to study philosophy. From 28 to 66, he explains philosophy's rewards to a wider audience, a friendly "tu," which certainly includes Maecenas. To illustrate his precepts, he gives several examples of unphilosophical and therefore unhappy men. In 67–90 Horace develops his worst bad example: the "Populus Romanus" (67), changeable and rootless, frantically active, never finding satisfaction. This section contains some strong satire, but returns to the calm instruction of the second part. In his conclusion, 91–105, Horace once again addresses Maecenas specifically and reaffirms their friendship.

Readers of the imitation will detect these approximately corresponding divisions: 1–54, 55–119, 120–60, and 161–88. There is a certain amount of overlapping. Lines 48–54 cover the same material as the epistle's 28–32 (which begin its second part), but Pope does not address the general reader, his "tu," until line 55. Line 110 in his second section is the counterpart of Horace's 67, the first line of *his* third part, but we do not sense a new beginning at 110, since lines 101–19 form a coherent passage concerning King George. At line 120 Pope turns to the fickle people, Horace's subject beginning with the Latin 67. However, despite the overlapping, imitation and source have basically parallel structures.

In 1–54 Pope follows Horace in explaining, to Bolingbroke, his decision to take up philosophy. Although he appears to consider becoming "Sometimes a Patriot, active in debate" (27), action is not a serious possibility here. The line occurs in a passage, 23–34, closely modeled on the Latin 13–19, a brief survey of different schools of philosophy. Horace considers both action (16–17) and inaction (18–19), as does Pope, who can see the attractiveness of "win[ning] my way by yielding to the tyde" (34). The point of both passages is the same: Pope and Horace wish to be eclectic, to be "Sworn to no Master" (24) in their philosophic studies.

Several small changes make Pope's affirmation of philosophy appear even more serious than Horace's in the original. Early in the epistle (2–6) Horace likens himself to a retired gladiator, the Roman equivalent of an ex-pug with cauliflower ears, but Pope omits this vulgar comparison, carrying over the martial connotation by referring to "Our Gen'rals" (7).[9] In his line 20 Horace compares himself, eager to begin philosophy, to an amorous, anxious man waiting all night for a girl who promised to come but lied. Pope gets rid of the frivolous lie and, by changing the eager lover's gender, distances himself from the example: "Long as the Night to her whose love's away" (36). He introduces a solemn couplet on the need for philosophical study that Horace's "Condo & compono" (12) ("gather and accumulate") barely suggests: "To lay this harvest up, and hoard with haste / What ev'ry day will want, and most, the last" (21–22).

So Pope will commence the study of philosophy. However, in his 1–27 Horace not only elects philosophy, but renounces poetry; he does not precisely specify the genre, but undoubtedly means lyric, referring to his Odes, the work of the maturity of his career.[10] Pope is more explicit about the kinds of poetry he wants to renounce; these, however, do *not* include the kinds he has recently been writing: satire and didactic verse. In 13–16 he is warned by a wise inner voice:

> "Friend Pope! be prudent, let your Muse take breath,
> "And never gallop Pegasus to death;

"Lest stiff, and stately, void of fire, or force,
"You limp, like Blackmore, on a Lord Mayor's horse."

As an ironic comparison to himself, Pope offers the sad example of the modern epic bard. Both the jocularity and the genre seem irrelevant to Pope's recent work. So does his replacing Horace's unnamed " 'senescentem . . . equum' " (8) not only with " 'Lord Mayor's horse,' " but with the overused flourish of " 'Pegasus' "; this alludes to the poetry most intimately tied to inspiration: epic and lyric. The following couplet, moreover, strongly implies by "rhymes and rattles" that Pope is only promising to write no more of what, in fact, he had not written since his poetic youth: "Farewell then Verse, and Love, and ev'ry Toy, / The rhymes and rattles of the Man or Boy" (17–18). Thus, in his poem's first section, he seems to be evading the question of whether he will cease to write.

When reading his second section, then, we may be inclined to think that his decision to drop poetry for philosophy was a mere feint. For while the reasoned address of the Latin epistle's 28–66 contains only a few mild satiric touches, Pope's lines 55–120 attack his usual targets, not excepting the king:

> Be furious, envious, slothful, mad or drunk,
> Slave to a Wife or Vassal to a Punk,
> A Switz, a High-dutch, or a Low-dutch Bear—
> All that we ask is but a patient Ear.
>
> (61–64)

Maynard Mack quotes this passage, which obviously refers to George's German background, his dominating wife, and his equally dominating mistress, as a particularly clear example of Pope's use of political innuendo. Further on, Pope levels the same weapon at Walpole. Playing on Horace's *"murus aheneus"* (57) ("barrier of bronze," a metaphor for a good conscience), he produces: "Be this thy Screen, and this thy Wall of Brass; / Compar'd to this, a Minister's an Ass" (95–96). Opposition journalists, Mack shows, often associated Walpole with brass and with screens and screening evildoers.[11]

As the second section ends, in 101–19, Pope attacks George with satire that would be apparent even to someone ignorant of the opposition's innuendo. The passage begins with a worldly voice, meant perhaps to oppose the inner voice of lines 13–16, advocating the pursuit of " 'Place and Wealth' " (103); so does a similar voice in

Horace's 62–63. However, when Pope counters this unsavory doctrine, he departs from his source in order to invest George, already characterized as easily controlled by others, with shrill and fatuous impotence. Horace alludes to the Roman theater, in which the Roscian law reserved for the wealthy order of knights good seats— all to see the "lacrymosa Poemata Pupi" (64). Pope replaces Pupius's dreadful "teary plays" with opera sung by castrati, among whom he seems to place the king. An Englishman who acquires "'Place and Wealth'" can, for his pains, "have a Box where Eunuchs sing, / And foremost in the Circle eye a King" (105–6).

Then Pope recasts Horace's fable about the fox and the lion. If asked by the "Populus Romanus" why he does not share their opinions, "judiciis," as he does their colonnades, "porticibus" (67–68), Horace would answer as the wise fox answered the lion when invited into his cave: "'Quia me vestigia terrent / Omnia te adversum spectantia, nulla retrorsum'" (71–72) ("'Because these footprints make me afraid, / all of them going in towards you, none coming back out'"). He means that he does not want to think as everyone else does. His is the lion of popular opinion. Pope responds not to the people in general, but to the "well-drest Rabble" and "S*z" (Schutz, a court functionary) (111–12); to these he would "give the answer Reynard gave, / 'I cannot like, Dread Sir! your Royal Cave'" (114–15). His is a royal lion. Finally, to the fable Pope adds a moral without equivalent in the source: "Adieu to Virtue if you're once a Slave: / Send her to Court, you send her to her Grave" (118–19).

So there is plentiful satire in the imitation's second section, enough—if it contained nothing significant but satire—to convince us that Pope really does not intend to give up this kind of writing. However, there is also a current of doubt regarding the value of satire. At the very beginning, Pope expresses a motif familiar to readers of the *Imitations*—lack of conviction that satire will have any significant effect:

> Say, does thy blood rebel, thy bosom move
> With wretched Av'rice, or as wretched Love?
> Know, there are Words, and Spells, which can controll
> (Between the Fits) this Fever of the soul:
> Know, there are Rhymes, which (fresh and fresh apply'd)
> Will cure the arrant'st Puppy of his Pride.
>
> (55–60)

"Between the Fits," between its parentheses, has the effect of an instinctual warning rising up to disturb the speaker as he recommends what might be either philosophy or satire. ("Words, and Spells" renders *"verba & voces"* [34], by which Horace means the healing doctrines of philosophy.) The second parenthesis seems more of a conscious comment, this time about unquestionably satiric "Rhymes" (thus rendering *"piacula"* [36], synonymous with *"verba & voces"*), but the result is the same for readers.[12] We question the worth of these "Words," "Spells," and "Rhymes": they control only intermittently (and when least needed—between fits) and must be always newly made.

At this point, in the previously quoted lines 61–64, Pope focuses on the king, that "Slave" and "Vassal." To say now "All that we ask is but a patient Ear" (64) merely lays ironic stress on the impossibility of getting dull George, whose resistance to poetry is an old subject for Pope, to listen to *either* philosophy *or* satire. Perhaps we pity the weary satirist, trapped by his vocation in the endless task of fashioning and applying fresh rhymes that he who needs them most will never hear.

Pope strongly doubts the effectiveness of satire. Moreover, he is attracted by philosophy. One passage in the second section, in fact, recommends the philosophic life with such appeal that we may be less inclined to pity a ceaselessly rhyming satirist than to doubt his sanity. Lines 65–76 constitute a magnificent translation of the Latin 41–48, which oppose vain ambition to philosophic calm. The English passage concludes with a plea that seems to me more heartfelt than anything in the Latin:

> Wilt thou do nothing for a nobler end,
> Nothing, to make Philosophy thy friend?
> To stop thy foolish views, thy long desires,
> And ease thy heart of all that it admires?
>
> (73–76)[13]

Pope urges the reader "to make Philosophy thy friend," to become, in effect, a philosopher. When he speaks as a satirist in this second section, however, he seems not to have taken his own advice. His satire is angry, and so the satirist is likely to be angry and to lack tranquility. He will certainly be busy, with his "Rhymes . . . (fresh and fresh apply'd)," as busy in his way as the Merchant, foolishly "Scar'd at the spectre of pale Poverty," who flies "to either India" (70, 69). Therefore, considering the somewhat doubtful prospect that satire will do much good, one may ask why a passion for writing it is any better than another man's passion for money? Could not the satirist's intention of reforming others be, in fact, a "foolish view"?

Possibly Pope seeks to resolve the opposition of satire and philosophy, if only for a moment, by combining satirist and philosopher in a single virtue-embodying figure. Would you not, he asks, welcome an adviser

> . . . who bids thee face with steddy view
> Proud Fortune, and look shallow Greatness thro':
> And, while he bids thee, sets th' Example too?
>
> (107–9)

However, this counselor seems less devoted to satire than to philosophy. Pope's triplet is firmly based on Horace's 65–66, the climax of his second section. Here the ideal philosopher (or philosophy personified) is one "qui Fortunae te responsare superbae / Liberum & erectum, *praesens* hortatur, & aptat" ("who tells you to defy proud fortune / by standing straight and free, who always helps you"). Horace lacks an equivalent for "shallow Greatness," and we know what Pope means by that. Nonetheless, "look through" is not a synonym for "write against."

Finally, despite the strength of Pope's attack on the king in 110–19, the second section's conclusion, these same lines obliquely recommend, through contrast with the source, a strict retirement that suits the philosopher better than the satirist. *Epist.* 1.1 speaks of the unenlightened "Populus Romanus" wondering why Horace shares none of their opinions, as he does their colonnades ("ut porticibus" [68]) in Rome. He visits Rome, but Pope does not visit London. A disembodied "Doctrine, in St. James's Air" (110) offends fashionable citizens, and "honest S*z" is scandalized by a "spark" (112), admittedly an ambiguous term, but less likely to designate Pope himself, no spark, than a fiery particle of his satire. Pope routinely associates retirement with virtue, which, of course, a satirist must have. But the contrast with Horace suggests that he lacks the will to confront or even observe vice, which is centered in London, at the court.

The suggestion is indirect, because there is no direct contrast: Horace surely has no intention of presenting himself as a satirist who opposes the court of Augustus. He does not enjoy meeting his fellow citizens in Rome, but the court, represented here by Maecenas, always remains for him the source of the rational leadership that keeps the "Populus Romanus" in order. While Horace does not mention Augustus himself, perhaps the emperor contributes to Pope's satire, since we are likely to think of this strong ruler when Pope sneers at George's impotence and his willingness to be manipulated.

The first couplet of the imitation's third section (120–60) also suggests that the emperor may be an exemplar for Pope: "Well, if a King's a Lion, at the least / The People are a many-headed Beast." Although the epistle mentions only the people, "*Bellua multorum est capitum*" (73) ("The beast has many heads"), "King's" directs our minds to Augustus, and we know Horace's consistent perspective on him: that truly royal lion gives his people leadership. This makes it all the more apparent that by not leading *his*, George allows them to go off in a variety of directions, all bad. He ushers them into the depravity Pope soon describes:

> Their Country's wealth our mightier Misers drain,
> Or cross, to plunder Provinces, the Main:
> The rest, some farm the Poor-box, some the Pews;
> Some keep Assemblies, and wou'd keep the Stews;
> Some with fat Bucks on childless Dotards fawn;
> Some win rich Widows by their Chine and Brawn;
> While with the silent growth of ten per cent,
> In Dirt and darkness hundreds stink content.
>
> (126–33)

The focus is wide at the beginning (the country, the provinces), for the corrupting force, coming down from the court, exerts itself upon the nation as a whole. Then, as the focus narrows, the animality of legacy-hunters is emphasized by associating the "fat Bucks" they give as presents with their own "Chine and Brawn." Finally we look into a dark recess, perhaps a metamorphosis of the "'Royal Cave,'" of line 115; if it is that, a vivid lesson is being given in what happens to those who enter there, as the "Grave" for virtue becomes a teeming womb for vice. In any case, Pope signals the corruption of the human spirit by showing mankind, deeply fallen, as grubs or insects.

Of this passage Frank Stack writes: "There is nothing like this in Horace's poem, indeed nothing like it in the whole of Horace, except perhaps in the last Roman ode. . . . The moral fervour and bitter cynicism here are all Pope's own."[14] In fact, the equivalent Latin passage, attacking a variety of mercenary schemers, is unusually dark:

> Pars hominum gestit conducere *Publica*. Sunt qui
> Crustis & *Pomis*, Viduas venentur avaras,

Excipiantque Senes quos in vivaria mittunt.
Multis occulto crescit res faenore—

(74–77)

(Some men like contracting with the government, others hunt
for rich old ladies they pursue with applies and with crusts,
or trap old gentlemen in snares to put in private zoos.
Many make secret loans and reap the interest. . . .)

But Stack is right. Compared to the repellent physicality of "fat
Bucks" and "Chine and Brawn," there is almost something funny
in the conceit of treating senior citizens like pets or zoo animals.
Though gripped by a passion for money, at least Horace's characters escape the dehumanizing depths of "Dirt and darkness." We
know the reason, or are made aware when reading epistle and
imitation together: Augustus and his court limit the consequences
of the ugly practices—crooked contracting, legacy-hunting, and
usury—that Horace condemns.

Therefore, we are not surprised when Horace becomes more
tolerant and makes his targets not villains but fickle fools who hurt
only themselves: rich men who change their minds about where to
build their estates or whether to be married or not, poor men just as
changeable (80–90). Horace is teaching again, by giving us satiric
examples. But one is surprised when Pope changes in the same way.
For in lines 134–60 he uses similar examples—wealthy Sir Job and
Flavio, poor men collectively—and in the same way. He follows
Horace by placing satire in the service of philosophy, which here
takes an ascendancy it will not relinquish.

But in the imitation's second part Pope is both upset and angry
when showing us how the court, which should, like the Augustan
court, give real leadership, functions as the source of corruption.
Then the third part opens with a shocking picture of how far this
extends and of its capacity for "silent growth." "In Dirt and
darkness hundreds stink content" echoes most unpleasantly the
Epistle to Bathurst on the "Riches" that "like insects, when con-
ceal'd they lie, / Wait but for wings, and in their season, fly" (171–
72). So the future promises to be even worse than the present. The
moment in the poem at which this ominous prospect becomes most
clear may seem an inappropriate point for Pope to begin a withdrawal into philosophic calm.

However, if one considers the entire imitation, one will consider
this development, abrupt though it is, as a reasonable conclusion to
Pope's dialogue between public concerns and personal needs. The

poet is a veteran who reposes in the "Sabbath of my days"; now he contemplates the "last" of his "labours" (1–3). The philosophic life attracts him strongly. He shows his awareness of the futility of further struggle: no one wants to listen to him, neither king nor subjects, who, at their worst, as Pope shows in a final explosion of ire, have virtually lost touch with their own humanity. He has good reason, then, to try to save himself, his spiritual self, rather than this unsavable world. While in the imitation of *Epist.* 2.2 the prospect of withdrawal troubles him because it may be selfish, the same concern seems not to trouble him here, in part, perhaps, because he intends to share a retirement with Bolingbroke.

In his last section (161–84), Pope demonstrates self-possession, good humor, and a philosophic mind, just as Horace does in the equivalent 91–105. Even the reference to the hygiene of Lady Mary (164) is mild compared to remarks under this head elsewhere, and in this context Pope is claiming to be less than tidy himself. Following Horace in his imagined dialogue with Maecenas, Pope directs most of the gentle satire here at himself and Bolingbroke: the first disorganized in dress and thought (he says), the second wrongly attentive to the outer disarray, not the inner (161–76). Pope also follows Horace in the purpose of his satire: to show the need for philosophy.

And, again like Horace, he seems to bring himself physically before his correspondent, dispensing with the epistolary convention of distance, observed in the beginnings of both poems. Horace, however, imagines an unplanned meeting with Maecenas in Rome, in "porticibus," when both have other business: "Si curtatus *inaequali* tonsore capillos / Occurro, rides" (91–92) ("After an unbalanced barber has given me a trimming, / if we meet, you laugh"). At this point in the imitation, however, there are no references to London, from which, in lines 110–19, Pope insists on keeping his distance. We can safely assume that he envisions his conversation with Bolingbroke as taking place at Twickenham; he is probably anticipating St. John's arrival from France, which occurred in July 1738, soon after this poem was written. As in the very first of the *Imitations of Horace,* Twickenham accepts, this time in prospect, this best of "Statesmen, out of Place."

The difference in location subtly reminds us how the relationship between Pope and Bolingbroke differs from that between Horace and Maecenas. Pope is the host; Bolingbroke an exile, however elegant, without a place in England. But while Horace can criticize Maecenas as an inadequate philosopher who pays too much attention to appearances, he shows a proper subordinate's regard for one of exalted rank. He begins this poem by addressing Maecenas specifically as his patron: "*Prima* dicte mihi, summa dicende Camena!" ("My very first Muse sang of you, as will my very last"). Pope writes rather generally of "labours past" that St. John's "love indulg'd." Now Horace reaffirms his dependence: "De *te pendentis, te suspicientis*, Amici" (102) (the poet is "the friend who depends on you and on your good advice").

Although he can give Maecenas moral counsel, the poet depends on him for both economic support and advice about the world, which has witnessed the minister's great success. But Bolingbroke can confer no patronage on Pope and for more than twenty years has not notably prospered in the world. Perhaps, the implication goes, he should depend on Pope's advice in that quarter. At any rate, the imitation's rendering of the Latin 102 obviously refers to philosophical, rather than worldly, "Wisdom": "[Bolingbroke] ought to make me (what he can, or none,) / That Man divine whom Wisdom calls her own" (179–80). Thus, the imitation appears to reverse the relationship between poet and addressee that exists in *Epist.* 1.1.

As a result, Pope confers on his friend an encomium Maecenas does not receive in the source, for Bolingbroke is obviously the basis of the idealized figure of 181–84, one who is great despite his worldly lack of success:

> Great without Title, without Fortune bless'd,
> Rich ev'n when plunder'd, honour'd while oppress'd,
> Lov'd without youth, and follow'd without power,
> At home tho' exil'd, free, tho' in the Tower.

Horace could not bestow such paradoxical praises, loosely related to the "Stoic paradoxes" he plays with in 103–5, on Maecenas, who is great with title (or at least with high rank), rich with fortune, honored, but certainly not oppressed. Thus the imitation emphasizes the exemplary moral superiority of St. John to Maecenas. But it also emphasizes his lack of stature and strength (the mention of the Tower, where he had not been imprisoned, may even serve to remind him of his enemies' power), and thus makes attractive to him the philosophical retreat I believe Pope is advising.

We may wonder why a man of such fortitude, so naturally gifted, it may seem, with the qualities of a philosopher, needs such a retreat. But Pope suggests that Bolingbroke has imperfections even as, after the noble description of 181–84, the imitation seems to rise yet higher in his praise:

> In short, that reas'ning, high, immortal Thing,
> Just less than Jove, and much above a King,
> Nay half in Heav'n—
>
> (185–87)

The businesslike "In short" and the nebulous "Thing" (trailing a string of honorific adjectives) clash with the sentiments. "Just less than Jove" is ridiculous, and "much above a King," if we think of George, another bit of teasing; finally, "half in heaven" uneasily suspends St. John between angel and man. Rather than leave him there, the poem concludes by letting him fall back to earth:

> except (what's mighty odd)
> A Fit of Vapours clouds this Demi-god.
>
> (187–88)

Like Pope's 185–88, Horace's conclusion follows a suspect climax with a definite anticlimax:

> Ad summam, *Sapiens* uno minor est *Jove!* Dives!
> Liber! honoratus! pulcher!—
> —Rex denique regum!
> Praecipue sanus—
> —Nisi cum pituita molesta est.
>
> (103–5)

(A final word: the wise man stands just below Jove: wealthy, free, famous, handsome; a king, in other words, of kings. Above all, he's sane, unless, that is, he has a cold.)

However, the satire falls not upon Maecenas, but upon the ideal sage of the Stoics, whose paradoxical teachings Horace ridicules elsewhere. Here he delights in lowering their paragon, seized by the nose, to merely human rank.

One purpose is shared by the poets: to establish as an extreme opposed to the aimlessness and worse of ordinary humanity an impossible and rather stuffy ideal of virtue, perhaps no less distant from the desirable mean. Pope obviously does not mean that his friend actually represents that faulty ideal, as the Stoic sage does; at most, Bolingbroke is being warned against a tendency to posture like the sage, forgetting that he is "lov'd" for his human warmth and charm. In each poem poet and noble addressee stand together as members of a small company of realistic, reasonable men prepared to find philosophy rewarding. Nonetheless, because Pope brings his friend, rather than a third party, down to earth, he reminds Bolingbroke of his humanity, his fallibility.

Perhaps Pope specifically intended to advise Bolingbroke that to be spiritually, perhaps even physically, free, he had best forget all political aspirations. With one "half in Heav'n," the other half, Pope may have thought, was too busy on earth; although Bolingbroke praised retirement in his correspondence, his political ambitions seem to have died hard. In the judgment of H. T. Dickinson, at about the time this imitation was written, although "nearly sixty. . . . despite himself, [Bolingbroke] betrayed his yearning for a political comeback."[15] Perhaps "Why will you break the Sabbath of my days?" (3) refers to a proposal that Pope involve himself, if only in a peripheral way, in some political stratagem he felt neither he nor Bolingbroke should undertake.

Only a few years earlier, in 1736, Swift had expressed in a letter his fears concerning the "Health" and "fortune," of Bolingbroke, "so long a Squanderer of both." Pope replied that their friend "in the whole turn of his letters" seemed "to be a settled and principled Philosopher." However, he also commented, in a telling aside: "The world will certainly be the better for this change of life." Obviously he thought that Bolingbroke would be the better for it too. Judging from Swift's concern, as well as Dickinson's observation, Pope may have believed he needed reminding.[16] Of course it is conceivable that Bolingbroke realized his career was over, and that he would never regain power, whether or not Walpole lost it. In this case, Pope's purpose would be consolatory, to reconcile him to the fate of a philosophical life all the more attractive because they can share it.

Frank Stack correctly discerns an "intensity" in Pope's feeling for his old friend, but I do not agree that its source is simply Pope's insistence that Bolingbroke "make me . . . / That Man divine whom Wisdom calls her own."[17] As much or more intensity comes out of Pope's concern for Bolingbroke. Of course, Pope too has earned his retirement, as he insists at the beginning. Lines 165–70, which express the confusion of his thoughts, show that he needs it, but the failure of St. John to be alarmed at this confusion in Pope shows that St. John's own mental state is probably more disordered. The entire imitation, moreover, exposes the futility of continuing to fight, not only as a satirist, but also as a politician, against a corrupting court and a corrupted people.

At the end of the poem Pope looks forward to a future at Twickenham, away from the world, shared by two of philosophic mind. Although neither is young and both are male, this conclusion is analogous to the union of lovers with which comedies often conclude. In fact, in both its general structure and several particular features, this imitation is remarkably close to the comic archetype outlined by Northrop Frye. It differs from that, however, in a detail doubly significant because here Pope also differs from Horace.[18]

The First Epistle of the First Book of Horace Imitated begins in separation; although Pope seems annoyed by Bolingbroke's request for verse, the source of the real separation between them is unjust "paternal" authority of the kind Frye finds in comedy. In this imitation it is embodied in the king and court that drove Bolingbroke from Pope, and from his rightful high place in England, into exile across the channel, while forcing Pope into something similar at Twickenham. Both should be together as part of England's court. George, Walpole, and the actual court's "well-drest Rabble" are "obstructing characters . . . in charge of the play's society," and surely Pope's "audience recognizes that they are usurpers," especially since Pope reminds us of the king's foreign origin and attachments.[19] Finally, the presence of Maecenas in the source, with Augustus standing behind him, and of Bolingbroke in the imitation gives us additional assurance that the wrong people are in charge.

At the poem's end, philosophical retirement—not the old duty to oppose—has brought Pope and Bolingbroke together in something quite like the "pragmatically free society" that Frye finds in existence at the end of a comedy.[20] In the comradely state that Pope anticipates, no one could seem freer from inner demands, from outside pressures. However, the comedy is not quite complete:

> The tendency of comedy is to include as many people as possible in its final society: the blocking characters are more often reconciled or converted than simply repudiated.[21]

In this imitation the "blocking characters" are king, court, and, in a secondary position, the people, too depraved for salvation by good politics or good poetry. In short, Pope and Bolingbroke have been blocked by the world, which Twickenham does not include. To be happy, to be free, Pope and Bolingbroke must shut that world out, but readers cannot shut it out of their thoughts.

Comparison with comedy will not be of much help in elucidating the Horatian source. Nothing of substance separates Maecenas from Horace, for whom paternal authority is certainly just; Maecenas represents it, in fact. There are no blocking characters to convert. However, even though the structure of the whole is not really comic, the final encounter of Horace and Maecenas is dramatically poised, like a scene in a play, and their stage is vastly crowded compared to that occupied by Bolingbroke and Pope.

First, they are in Rome, the teeming streets, surrounded by the "Populus Romanus." Moreover, nothing Horace says implies that his patron, this powerful Augustan politician, should retire with him to the Sabine farm, which Maecenas was never known to visit, or to any other retreat. Horace encourages Maecenas to study philosophy, yes, and suggests that he needs it. So he recommends to every reader of the poem, to the generalized, rational "tu." All wise men cannot retire from the world, but can learn to live virtuously nonetheless. Maecenas can do this in the court of Augustus. What better place? As for Horace, though residing in the country, which *he* will leave upon occasion, he is still a part of the single order of Augustan society. Unlike Pope and Bolingbroke, Horace and Maecenas remain in the world. The world is their stage.

How small has the second order become! This is what the final contrast helps readers to see. Pope's poem ends with the ultimate expression of the theme of refuge that shows up in the *Imitations* from the first, in which the bold satirist engaged vice and folly from Twickenham, to this, the last. His second order is finally a vision of a society of two persons, with no connections to the world.

Of course, this leaves no one visible to fight against the aimless, destructive power there. In earlier poems Pope has shown that this power can disturb him; the pretense here is that he and Bolingbroke can have peace. In fact, the administration press was provoked by the political satire in this imitation into attacking Pope.[22] But nothing in it anticipates any reprisals. Pope does not foresee a continued struggle because, as in both his imitation of *Epist.* 1.6 and the *Epilogue to the Satires,* with its final note, he is, while firing his most lethal shots, retiring from the field. The shots have no significant effect, Pope seems to believe, and nothing else seems available to arrest the disintegrative forces at work. Retirement with Bolingbroke is a delightful prospect, but nothing about it will stave off the general collapse that Pope has seen coming for years and that, he knows, will involve him too:

> Yet, yet a moment, one dim Ray of Light
> Indulge, dread Chaos, and eternal Night!
> Of darkness visible so much be lent,
> As half to show, half veil the deep Intent.
> Ye Pow'rs! whose Mysteries restor'd I sing,
> To whom Time bears me on his rapid wing,
> Suspend a while your Force inertly strong,
> Then take at once the Poet and the Song.
>
> (*Dunciad,* 4.1–8)

Appendix
Epilogue to the Satires: Farewell to Horace

In dialogue 1 of the *Epilogue to the Satires,* a "Friend" from court complains of Pope's satire: "the Court sees nothing in 't" (2). He advocates the example of Horace—as he conceives of him:

> But *Horace,* Sir, was delicate, was nice;
> *Bubo* observes, he lash'd no sort of *Vice:*
> *Horace* would say, *Sir* Billy *serv'd the Crown,*
> Blunt *could do Bus'ness,* H——ggins *knew the Town,*
> In *Sappho* touch the *Failing of the Sex,*
> In rev'rend Bishops note some *small Neglects,*
> And own, the *Spaniard* did a *waggish thing,*
> Who cropt our Ears, and sent them to the King.
> His sly, polite, insinuating stile
> Could please at Court, and make Augustus smile:
> An artful Manager, that crept between
> His Friend and Shame, and was a kind of *Screen.*
>
> (11–22)

Do these lines "reflect," as Weinbrot argues, "Pope's calm judgment" (*AC,* p. 140)? How could they? Obviously, "Pope does not give this account of Horace in his own person, but puts it into the mouth of the pusillanimous and time-serving 'Friend' whose opinions in the poem he seeks to refute and ridicule almost all the way down the line."[1] Before this "account" is given, the Friend has already shown his ignorance concerning the *Imitations of Horace.* He seems not even to know what an imitation is, since, before charging Pope with being insufficiently Horatian, he accuses him of stealing from Horace (6–7). The two examples he then gives of Pope's supposed plagiarism, both from the first of the *Imitations,* are very far from the parallel lines in the Horatian text.[2]

The real interest in the characterization of Horace as a contemptible sycophant lies in Pope's lack of response to it. For

Horace disappears from the poem (from both Dialogue 1 and Dialogue 2) as the Friend proceeds without a break from his Walpolean version of the Augustan satirist, who acts as a *"Screen,"* to the Great Man himself: "Go see Sir Robert," he advises (27). Here, not before, an angered Pope interrupts, to speak of Walpole, not Horace. Pope knows the Friend—his enemy—knows how shallow he is: had the Friend wanted to flatter, he would have joined the coterie in *Arbuthnot* who tell the weary poet that "I cough like *Horace.*" Obviously Pope sees no point in defending to such a man the moral satirist whom for years, though never in any simple fashion, he made his alter ego.

Just as obviously, there is no point in imitating Horace. Pope does imitate *Sat.* 2.3 at the very beginning of Dialogue 1 in order to link the Friend with Damasippus, who impudently criticizes Horace in that *sermo;* therefore, here Pope links himself with Horace. But the poet's note indicating the Horatian allusion firmly promises that it will be the last: "These two lines are from Horace [*Sat.* ii.iii.1–4]; and the only lines that are so in the whole Poem." Pope keeps his promise, and little wonder. Neatly applying lines from the *sermones* to his own age would not impress his enemies at court even if they bothered to compare Latin to English, for they see Horace in their own image. Differing from the Latin text, the means by which Pope creates the most significant meaning in the *Imitations,* is certain to have no effect. By creating gaps, he invites the reader to participate, but the reader need not participate. The remarks of the Friend in lines 1–10 suggest that he and others like him are most unlikely to detect gaps.

Horace will gain Pope nothing, and, after the first two lines, the *Epilogue to the Satires* is *Something Like Horace,* its subtitle, only in being a dialogue. I would hesitate before calling it Juvenalian or Persian, however, and it does at least exhibit Pope's concern, so characteristic of the *Imitations of Horace,* with both the value and the risk of satire. Horace will gain him nothing, but the un-Horatian stratagems of the *Epilogue* seem able to gain him no more. Nothing can affect men so dull as the Friend—no combination of wit, irony, scatology, and indignation. So Pope plainly recognizes in his final note, probably written, according to Butt (p. xxxix), in 1743:

This was the last poem of the kind printed by our author, with a resolution to publish no more; but to enter thus, in the most plain and solemn manner he could, a sort of PROTEST against that insuperable corruption and depravity of manners, which he had been so unhappy as to live to see. Could he have hoped to have amended any, he had continued those attacks; but bad men were grown so shameless and so powerful, that Ridicule was become as unsafe as it was ineffectual. The Poem raised him, as he knew it would, some enemies; but he had reason to be satisfied with the approbation of good men, and the testimony of his own conscience.

Notes

Chapter 1. Reading the Imitation

1. *Lives of the English Poets,* ed. George Birbeck Hill, 3 vols. (Oxford: Clarendon Press, 1905), 3 : 246–47.

2. For examples, see R. E. Hughes, "Pope's *Imitations of Horace* and the Ethical Focus," *Modern Language Notes* 71 (1956): 569–74; Mary Lascelles, "Johnson and Juvenal," in *New Light on Dr. Johnson: Essays on the Occasion of His 250th Birthday,* ed. Frederick W. Hilles (New Haven: Yale University Press, 1959), pp. 35–55.

3. When Samuel Johnson "set down his imitation of the *Third Satire,* he mentally confronted not only the original Juvenalian lines . . . but the massive scholarship which interpreted their meanings and structural patterns" (Edward A. and Lillian D. Bloom, "Johnson's *London* and Its Juvenalian Texts," *Huntington Library Quarterly* 34 [1970]: 12). See also by these authors, "Johnson's *London* and the Tools of Scholarship," *Huntington Library Quarterly* 34 (1971): 115–39. In *Pope's Horatian Poems* (Columbus: Ohio State University Press, 1966), Thomas E. Maresca often accounts for Pope's apparent departures from Horace as instances of his referring to "an expansion of his text" (p. 41); the source of this expansion was "the lore of the annotators" (p. 17). See also Frank Stack on Pope's use of Dacier's commentary on Horace in *Pope and Horace: Studies in Imitation* (Cambridge: Cambridge University Press, 1985), pp. 50, 52.

4. Aubrey L. Williams, "*Pope and Horace:* The Second Epistle of the Second Book," in *Restoration and Eighteenth-Century Literature: Essays in Honor of Alan Dugald McKillop,* ed. Carroll Camden (Chicago: University of Chicago Press, 1963), p. 310.

5. John Denham, Preface to *The Destruction of Troy,* in *The Poetical Works of Sir John Denham,* ed. Theodore Howard Banks (New Haven: Yale University Press, 1928), p. 160; cf. Dryden's dedication to the *Aeneis:* "I have endeavoured to make Virgil speak such English as he would himself have spoken, if he had been born in England, and in this present age" (*Essays of John Dryden,* ed. W. P. Ker, 2 vols. (New York: Russell and Russell, 1961), 2 : 228; Alexander Tytler, *Essay on the Principles of Translation* (London, 1791), p. 13.

6. Harold F. Brooks, "The 'Imitation' in English Poetry, Especially in Formal Satire, before the Age of Pope," *Review of English Studies* 25 (1949): 127.

7. George Steiner, *After Babel: Aspects of Language and Translation* (New York and London: Oxford University Press, 1975), p. 298.

8. Wolfgang Iser, "The Reading Process: A Phenomenological Approach," *New Literary History* 3 (1972): 285. The elements within narrative include "segments of characters, narrator, plot, and fictitious reader perspectives" (Iser, *The Act of Reading: A Theory of Aesthetic Response* [Baltimore: Johns Hopkins University Press, 1978], p. 197).

9. Iser, "Indeterminacy and the Reader's Response In Prose Fiction," in

Aspects of Narrative: Selected Papers from the English Institute, ed. J. Hillis Miller (New York: Columbia University Press, 1971), p. 14.

10. Howard D. Weinbrot, "Johnson's *London* and Juvenal's Third Satire: The Country as 'Ironic Norm'," *Modern Philology* 73 (Supplement, 1976): S65.

11. "There are, of course, limits to the reader's willingness to participate, and these will be exceeded if the text makes things too clear or, on the other hand, too obscure: boredom and overstrain represent the two poles of tolerance" (*Act of Reading,* p. 108).

12. See Weinbrot's *Augustus Caesar in "Augustan" England: The Decline of a Classical Norm* (Princeton: Princeton University Press, 1978).

13. See E.D. Hirsch, Jr., *Validity in Interpretation* (New Haven: Yale University Press, 1967), pp. 47–48.

14. John Butt, "Johnson's Practice in the Poetical Imitation," in *New Light on Dr. Johnson,* p. 31.

15. *The Poems of Samuel Johnson,* ed. David Nichol Smith and Edward L. McAdam, 2nd ed. (Oxford: Clarendon Press, 1974), p. 111. This edition is the source of subsequent quotations from *The Vanity of Human Wishes.*

16. R. Selden, "Dr. Johnson and Juvenal: A Problem in Critical Method," *Comparative Literature* 22 (1970): 299.

17. Charles E. Pierce, Jr., *The Religious Life of Samuel Johnson* (Hamden, Conn.: Archon Books, 1983), p. 114.

18. The Loeb translation:

> More still have been ruined by money too carefully amassed, and by fortunes that surpass all patrimonies by as much as the British whale exceeds the dolphin. It was for this that in the dire days Nero ordered Longinus and the great gardens of the over-wealthy Seneca to be put under siege; for this was it that the noble palace of the Laterani was beset by an entire cohort; it is but seldom that soldiers find their way into a garret! Though you carry but few plain silver vessels with you in a night journey, you will be afraid of the sword and cudgel of a freebooter, you will tremble at the shadow of a reed shaking in the moonlight; but the empty-handed traveller will whistle in the robber's face.
>
> The foremost of all petitions—the one best known to every temple—is for riches and their increase, that our money-chest may be the biggest in all the Forum. But you will drink no aconite out of an earthenware cup; you may dread it when a jewelled cup is offered you, or when Setine wine sparkles in a golden bowl.

19. Joel Weinsheimer, "'London'" and the Fundamental Problem of Hermeneutics," *Critical Inquiry* 9 (1982): 308.

20. Hirsch has recently modified his position on application, which "can be part of meaning" ("Meaning and Significance Reinterpreted," *Critical Inquiry* 11 [1984]: 212). But usually this is not the case: ". . . application is, after all, mainly concerned with the changing realm of significance" (215).

21. Weinsheimer, "'London,'" p. 321.

Chapter 2. Augustus

1. James William Johnson's "The Meaning of 'Augustan,'" *Journal of the History of Ideas* 19 (1958): 507–22 is substantially reproduced in his *Formation of English Neo-Classical Thought* (Princeton: Princeton University Press, 1967), pp. 16–30. Howard D. Weinbrot anticipated the anti-Augustan slant of his own 1978 book, to be discussed below, with his "History, Horace, and Augustus Caesar: Some Implications for Eighteenth-Century Satire, *Eighteenth Century Studies* 7

(1974): 391–414. Cf. Ian Watt, "Two Historical Aspects of the Augustan Tradition," in *Studies in the Eighteenth Century: Papers Presented at the David Nichol Smith Memorial Seminar, Canberra, 1966,* ed. R. F. Brissenden (Toronto: University of Toronto Press, 1968), pp. 67–79; Malcolm Kelsall, "Augustus and Pope," *Huntington Library Quarterly* 39 (1976): 117–31; Kelsall, "What God, What Mortal? The *Aeneid* and English Mock-Heroic," *Arion* 8 (1969): 359–79; Howard Erskine-Hill, "Augustans on Augustanism: England, 1655–1759," *Renaissance and Modern Studies* 11 (1967): 55–83. Kelsall's statement that during Pope's career "the virtues and vices of Augustanism were matters of active debate" ("Augustus and Pope," p. 119) expresses not only his position but approximately that of Watt and Erskine-Hill.

2. *Augustus Caesar in "Augustan" England: The Decline of a Cultural Norm* (Princeton: Princeton University Press, 1978). Quotations from this book, abbreviated *AC,* will be cited in the text.

3. James William Johnson and Ian Watt tie Augustus's fall from favor more closely to events in England. Johnson writes that the accession of George II, "christened George Augustus, irresistibly tempted the Tories to take the Whig title of 'Augustus' and subvert it to their own malicious ends" (*Formation,* p. 24). In Watt's judgment, Augustus's stock began to decline in 1714 with the arrival of the first George, after which the "Tories saw everything through darker spectacles, and consequently Augustus became both a tyrant in himself and the precursor of Rome's decline and fall" ("Two Historical Aspects," p. 75).

4. Erskine-Hill, *The Augustan Idea in English Literature* (London: Edward Arnold, 1983), p. 265.

5. *Augustan Idea,* p. 236n.

6. Joseph Spence, *Polymetis: or an Enquiry concerning the Agreement between the Works of the Roman Poets, and the Remains of the Antient Artists* (London, 1747), pp. 43, 20; Nathaniel Hooke, *The Roman History, from the Building of Rome to the Ruin of the Commonwealth,* 4th ed., 11 vols. (London, 1766–71), 11:438; Jonathan Swift, *A Discourse of the Contests and Dissentions between the Nobles and the Commons in Athens and Rome,* ed. Frank H. Ellis (Oxford: Clarendon Press, 1967), p. 111; Henry St. John Bolingbroke, *Remarks on the History of England,* in *The Works of the Late Honorable Henry St. John, Lord Viscount Bolingbroke,* ed. David Mallet, 5 vols. (1754; reprint ed., Hildesheim, W. Germany: Georg Olms, 1968), 1:310.

7. Spence, p. 20; Hooke, 7:344; Swift, pp. 100, 111. On the common belief that Roman despotism was inevitable after Sulla, see Oliver Goldsmith, *The History of Rome from the Foundation of the City of Rome to the Destruction of the Western Empire,* 2 vols. (London, 1827), 1:290; [François] Catrou and [Pierre] Rouillé, *The Roman History, with Notes Historical, Geographical, and Critical,* trans. R. Bundy, 6 vols. (London, 1728–37), 5:458; [Charles] Rollin and [Jean Baptiste Louis] Crévier, *The Roman History from the Foundation of Rome to the Battle of Actium,* trans. anon., 16 vols. (London, 1739–47), 10:247–48.

8. *Remarks on the History,* in *Works,* 1:293–94; *A Dissertation on Parties,* in *Works,* 2:182. One sign of the wide acceptance of the inevitability argument is its appearance in John Clarke's "Abridgement of the Roman History," a brief essay attached to Clarke's exceedingly popular Latin grammar (30 editions in the century), *An Introduction to the Making of Latin* (1721; reprint ed., Menston, England: Scolar Press, 1970). Clarke states that the Republic "fell by its own Power, which was occasion'd by the Ambition of the Leading Men, and the Civil Jars that arose from thence" (p. 218).

9. James William Johnson, *Formation,* pp. 61–62.

10. Mircea Eliade, *Cosmos and History: The Myth of the Eternal Return* (New York: Harper and Row, 1959), pp. 145–46. See also George H. Nadel, "Philosophy of History before Historicism," *History and Theory* 3 (1964): 298. For most in the seventeenth and eighteenth centuries the only movement in history that can be deemed cyclic is the return of nations to their own "first principles." Thus Samuel Johnson: "Every government, say the politicians, is perpetually degenerating toward corruption, from which it must be rescued at certain periods by the resuscitation of its first principles, and the re-establishment of its original constitution" (*The Rambler*, no. 156). The sources of this conception are Machiavelli and Polybius. Vico's influence in the period was negligible; see James Westfall Thompson and Bernard J. Holm, *A History of Historical Writing* (New York: MacMillan, 1942), 2:92–93.

11. *Letters on the Study and Use of History,* in *Works,* 2:287. For modern commentary, see George H. Nadel, "Philosophy of History"; Herbert Davis, "The Augustan Conception of History," in *Reason and the Imagination: Studies in the History of Ideas, 1600–1800,* ed. J. A. Mazzeo (New York: Columbia University Press, 1962), pp. 213–29; Thomas R. Preston, "Historiography as Art in Eighteenth-Century England," *Texas Studies in Literature and Language* 11 (1969): 1209–21.

12. See Isaac Kramnick, Introduction, *Historical Writings by Lord Bolingbroke,* ed. Isaac Kramnick (Chicago: University of Chicago Press, 1972), p. xi.

13. Johnson, *Formation,* p. 62.

14. *Augustan Idea,* pp. 213–14. Dryden's *Astraea Redux* is one of only five English poems known to Erskine-Hill that honor the restored king by comparing him to Augustus.

15. Vincent Carretta, *The Snarling Muse: Verbal and Visual Political Satire from Pope to Churchill* (Philadelphia: University of Pennsylvania Press, 1983), p. 105. On Pope and politics, see also Maynard Mack, *The Garden and the City: Retirement and Politics in the Later Poetry of Pope 1731–1743* (Toronto: University of Toronto Press, 1969), chapters 4, 5, and 6; Bertrand A. Goldgar, *Walpole and the Wits: The Relation of Politics to Literature, 1722–1742* (Lincoln, Nebraska: University of Nebraska Press 1976), pp. 122–33.

16. Mack, p. 128.

17. Johnson, *Formation,* p. 24; cf. Weinbrot, *AC,* p. 109. See note 3 on the king's name.

18. The quotation is from the *Craftsman,* no. 153 (7 July 1729), which characteristically compares Walpole to these personae while at the same time protesting, for the record, that no comparisons are intended. Further quotations from the *Craftsman* and other journals will be cited in the text; the source of some of the latter and for the *Craftsman* after 1738 is the *Gentleman's Magazine.* On the opposition's innuendo, see Mack, pp. 128–36, Goldgar, p. 43.

19. Mack, p. 138n.; *AC,* pp. 111–12.

20. *Craftsman* no. 7 (26 December 1726) and no. 121 (26 October 1728) refer to the maxim. No. 855 (15 November 1742) contains a letter headed "*The King* can do Wrong," which points out that the maxim did not save James II; the correspondent nonetheless admires the Hanoverians, "the present illustrious Family." Bolingbroke defends the maxim in the dedication, ironically addressed to Walpole, of his *Dissertation upon Parties.* Bolingbroke's Country Party professed its loyalty to the king; see H. T. Dickinson, *Bolingbroke* (London: Constable and Company, 1970), p. 200 and *Liberty and Property: Political Ideology in Eighteenth-Century Britain* (New York: Holmes and Meier, 1977), p. 180.

21. Although Walpole, not George, was the opposition's primary target, the

Imitations of Horace take, in my opinion, greater interest in the king than in the minister. But this should surprise no one unconvinced that Pope in the 1730s was a poetical adjunct to the *Craftsman.* Where kings are concerned, Pope shared with many others a vision that extended beyond politics into virtually metaphysical realms.

22. *Augustan Idea,* pp. 264–65.

23. See Watt, p. 75; Jay Arnold Levine, "Pope's *Epistle to Augustus,* Lines 1–30, *Studies in English Literature, 1500–1900* 7 (1967): 432.

24. *Works* 3:114, 115–16.

25. Hooke, 11:441. Following quotations from Hooke's *Roman History* and from Lyttelton's *Dialogues of the Dead* will be cited in the text.

Chapter 3. Horace

1. For the almost Christian Horace, see Thomas Maresca, *Pope's Horatian Poems* (Columbus: Ohio State University Press, 1966); Reuben Arthur Brower, *Alexander Pope: The Poetry of Allusion* (Oxford: Clarendon Press, 1959), pp. 163, 176.

2. "Epitaph For One who would not be buried in Westminster Abbey," in *The Twickenham Edition of the Poems of Alexander Pope,* vol. 6, *Alexander Pope: Minor Poems,* ed. Norman Ault and John Butt (New Haven: Yale University Press, 1954).

3. *The Correspondence of Alexander Pope,* ed. George Sherburn, 5 vols. (Oxford: Clarendon Press, 1956), 3:420.

4. *Augustan Idea,* p. 308.

5. In *Essays of John Dryden,* ed. W. P. Ker, 2 vols. (New York: Russell and Russell, 1961), 2:87, 78, 77.

6. Richard Hurd, *Q. Horatii Flacci, Epistolae ad Pisones et Augustum with an English Commentary and Notes,* 5th ed., 2 vols. (London, 1776), 2:42–43.

7. Lewis Crusius, *The Lives of the Roman Poets,* 3rd ed., 2 vols. (London, 1753), 1:67.

8. Ibid., 1:139–45, 127, 124.

9. See *Discourse, in Essays,* 2:85.

10. Joseph Warton, *An Essay on the Genius and Writings of Pope,* 2 vols. (1782; reprint ed., Farnborough, England: Gregg International, 1969), 2:345–46n.

11. Ibid., Cf. Thomas Blackwell, *Memoirs of the Court of Augustus,* 3 vols. (Edinburgh, 1753–63), 3:467–68.

12. *Essay,* 2:218; 1:171. It is interesting that, while Warton certainly understood that the *Aeneid* was intended to promote Augustus, he nonetheless gave Vergil's epic abundant praise for its beauty and grandeur; see the dedication (to Lyttelton) he wrote for Christopher Pitt's translation, *The Works of Virgil in Latin and English,* 4 vols. (London, 1753).

13. Spence, *Polymetis* (London, 1747), p. 21; George Lyttelton, *Dialogues of the Dead* (London, 1760), p. 100. Irony is certainly not intended in Lyttelton's dialogue. Horace gracefully accepts several compliments from Vergil, and the butt of the dialogue is Julius Caesar Scaliger, who makes a fool of himself by his haughty discourse toward both poets. When Mercury restores him to his senses (which he is said to have lost early in life), be becomes ashamed and submissive.

14. Crusius, 1:160; Spence, p. 21. Juvenal, of course, was often criticized for the obscenities, not of his life (of which nothing certain is known), but of his verse.

15. Lyttelton, p. 100; Lewis Maidwell, *An Essay upon the Necessity and Excel-*

lency of Education (1705; reprint ed., Los Angeles: Augustan Reprint Society, 1955), p. 13; Mary Wortley Montagu, The *Nonsense of Common Sense* (10 January 1738), in *Essays and Poems and Simplicity, A Comedy,* ed. Robert Halsband and Isobel Grundy (Oxford: Clarendon Press, 1977), p. 123; Crusius, 1:118; Rollin, *The History of the Arts and Sciences of the Antients,* trans. John Stacie, 4 vols. (London, 1739), 3:78; Richard Bentley, Latin dedication to his edition, *Q. Horatius Flaccus ex Recensione & cum Notis atque Emendationibus* (Cambridge, 1711). This dedication stresses Horace's excellence as a friend. Both Crusius (1:118) and Rollin (3:75–79) remind readers of the Roman tradition of friendship among unequals that allowed Horace his "frankness" (Rollin, 3:78) toward the great.

16. Abbé Le Moine d'Orgival, *Considerations sur l'Origine et le Progrès des Belles Lettres chez les Romains et les Causes de Leur Decadence* (Amsterdam, 1750), pp. 59–60, 61.

17. Warton, Introduction to Pitt's *Virgil,* p. xx; Lyttelton, pp. 100–101.

18. For background on the Horace-Juvenal question, see W. B. Carnochan, *Lemuel Gulliver's Mirror for Man* (Berkeley and Los Angeles: University of California Press, 1968), pp. 17–36; Harold Weber, " 'Comic Humour and Tragic Spirit': The Augustan Distinction between Horace and Juvenal," *Classical and Modern Literature* 1 (1981): 275–89.

19. Joseph Addison, *Poems on Several Occasions with a Dissertation upon the Roman Poets* (London, 1719), p. 49 (of the "Dissertation"); see John Dennis, *The Critical Works of John Dennis,* ed. Edward Niles Hooker, 2 vols. (Baltimore: Johns Hopkins University Press, 1939 and 1943), 1:226. Although Joseph Trapp would later express a preference for Juvenal, in 1718 he believed that favoring one satirist over the other was mostly a matter of *"Inclination" (The Preface to the Aeneis of Virgil* [1718; reprint ed., Los Angeles: Augustan Reprint Society, 1982]. p. ix).

20. *Discourse,* in *Essays,* 2:98–99.

21. Joseph Trapp, *Lectures on Poetry* (London, 1742), pp. 227, 224, 232, 235; Crusius, 2:88, 89.

22. Addison, *Dialogues upon the Usefulness of Ancient Medals,* in *The Miscellaneous Works of Joseph Addison,* ed. A. C. Guthkelch, 2 vols. (London: G. Bell and Sons, 1914), 2:309.

23. Lyttelton, pp. 112, 113.

24. (1730; reprint ed., Los Angeles: Augustan Reprint Society, 1968), p. 16. With Harte's *Essay* was printed a translation from Boileau, "A Discourse of Satires Arraigning Persons by Name," which praises Horace's satire for naming names. The obvious purpose is to give Pope implicit praise for doing the same. In the introduction to this reprint, Thomas B. Gilmore suggests that Pope himself, seeking the comparison with Horace, was the translator of Boileau (p. viii).

25. Cf. William Kupersmith's assertion that "the tradition of innocuousness which characterized the Horatian role provided ideal camouflage for the political satirist" ("Vice and Folly in Neoclassical Satire," *Genre* 11 [1978]: 56).

26. See Weinbrot, *AC,* pp. 142–49, 175–81. Cf. Goldgar on the "Juvenalian cast" to satire against Walpole *after* Pope's *Epilogue to the Satires* (*Walpole and the Wits: The Relation of Politics to Literature, 1722–1742* [Lincoln, Nebraska: University of Nebraska Press, 1976] p. 174).

27. Weinbrot, *Alexander Pope and the Traditions of Formal Verse Satire* (Princeton: Princeton University Press, 1982), p. 40.

28. Goldgar, p. 24.

29. In the translation of Joseph P. Clancy, *The Odes and Epodes of Horace* (Chicago: University of Chicago Press, 1960):

When a man is just and firm in his purpose,
the citizens burning to approve a wrong
or the frowning looks of a tyrant
do not shake his fixed mind.

Chapter 4. Reading Horace

1. Carolyn Goad, *Horace in the English Literature of the Eighteenth Century* (New Haven: Yale University Press, 1918), p. 7.

2. Spence, *Polymetis* (London, 1747), p. 287. On education in the classics, see my "Women, 'Learned Lumber,' and English Neoclassical Poetry," *Pacific Coast Philology* 15 (1980): 27–34.

3. Spence, *Observations, Anecdotes, and Characters of Books and Men,* ed. James M. Osborn, 2 vols. (Oxford: Clarendon Press, 1966), 1:13.

4. W. Y. Sellar, *The Roman Poets of the Augustan Age: Horace and the Elegiac Poets* (Oxford: Clarendon Press, 1892), pp. 2–3; Edward Kennard Rand, *The Building of Eternal Rome* (Cambridge, Mass.: Harvard University Press, 1943), p. 51.

5. Rand, p. 62; Crusius, *The Lives of the Roman Poets,* 3rd ed., 2 vols. (London, 1753), 1:xx.

6. See Ronald Paulson, "'Satire, and Poetry, and Pope,'" in *English Satire: Papers Read at a Clark Library Seminar, January 15, 1972* (Los Angeles: William Andrews Clark Memorial Library, 1972): Pope's "early non-satiric poetry [was] written during those years when he was making his Virgilian ascent from pastoral, georgic, and heroic epistle to epic, before settling in the 1730s in the foothills of the Horatian sermo and epistola" (p. 59).

7. All English renderings of the *sermones* are from my translation, *Horace's Satires and Epistles* (New York: W. W. Norton, 1977). In quoting, I have made occasional slight changes in the interest of literal accuracy.

8. *Aeneid* 6.756–853. This speech concludes:

"[R]emember, Roman, these will be your arts:
to teach the ways of peace to those you conquer,
to spare defeated peoples, tame the proud."

The translation is that of Alan Mandelbaum, *The Aeneid of Virgil* (Berkeley: University of California Press, 1971).

9. "Meaning and Significance Reinterpreted," *Critical Inquiry* 11 (1984): 209.

10. Ibid.

11. On what I have called "doubleness," see Fredric V. Bogel, *Acts of Knowledge: Pope's Later Poems* (Lewisburg, Pa.: Bucknell University Press, 1981), pp. 25–26; Thomas R. Edwards, Jr., *This Dark Estate: A Reading of Pope* (Berkeley and Los Angeles: University of California Press, 1963), pp. 81, 86; G. K. Hunter, "The 'Romanticism' of Pope's Horace," in *Essential Articles for the Study of Alexander Pope,* ed. Maynard Mack, rev. and enl. ed. (Hamden, Conn.: Archon, 1968), p. 592.

12. Edwards, p. 86.

13. Bogel, p. 25.

14. Warton, *An Essay on the Genius and Writings of Pope,* 2 vols. (1782; reprint ed., Westmead, England: Gregg International, 1969), 2:274.

15. Howard D. Weinbrot, *Alexander Pope and the Traditions of Formal Verse*

Satire (Princeton: Princeton University Press, 1982), p. 204; Howard Erskine-Hill, *Augustan Idea,* p. 295.

16. On the problems one may encounter in dealing with possible allusions, see Irvin Ehrenpreis, *Literary Meaning and Augustan Values* (Charlottesville, Va.: University Press of Virginia, 1974), pp. 8–16.

17. Erskine-Hill, p. 295.

Chapter 5. Beginning

1. For the immediate circumstances leading to Pope's imitating *Sat.* 2.1, see John Butt, Introduction, *The Twickenham Edition of the Poems of Alexander Pope,* vol. 4, *Alexander Pope: Imitations of Horace,* ed. John Butt, 2nd ed. (New Haven: Yale University Press, 1953), pp. xiii–xiv. This edition is the source of all quotations from the *Imitations of Horace* in both English and Latin. Pope's Latin texts occasionally differ in small details from standard texts of Horace. Whether individual variations are, in fact, editorial choices or simple oversights, they do not often seem important and will rarely be mentioned here.

2. For the poem and its printing history, see *The Twickenham Edition,* vol. 6, *Alexander Pope: Minor Poems,* ed. Norman Ault and John Butt (New Haven: Yale University Press, 1954).

3. *The First Epistle of the Second Book of Horace, Imitated,* lines 280–81.

4. For an enlightening discussion of Horace's strategy in this passage, see William S. Anderson, *Essays on Roman Satire* (Princeton: Princeton University Press, 1982), pp. 24–25.

5. The Twickenham edition prints the texts of the *sermones* in italics, with roman type used for emphasis. For the convenience of the reader, I am going to follow the example first set, as far as I know, by Aubrey L. Williams, of reversing this usage. See his "*Pope and Horace:* The Second Epistle of the Second Book," in *Restoration and Eighteenth-Century Literature,* ed. Carroll Camden (Chicago: University of Chicago Press, 1963), p. 311n.

6. Niall Rudd, *The Satires of Horace* (Cambridge: Cambridge University Press, 1966), p. 129; Edward P. Morris, ed., *Horace: Satires and Epistles* (1939; reprint ed., Norman, Okla.: University of Oklahoma Press, 1968), pp. 144–45. See also William S. Anderson, "Ironic Preambles and Satiric Self-Definition in Horace *Satire* 2.1," *Pacific Coast Philology* 19 (1984): 35–42.

7. See Thomas E. Maresca, *Pope's Horatian Poems* (Columbus: Ohio State University Press, 1966), pp. 37–72; Richard Steiger, "Pope's 'Augustan' Horace," *Arethusa* 10 (1977): 321–52; Frank Stack, *Pope and Horace: Studies in Imitation* (Cambridge: Cambridge University Press, 1985), pp. 29–59.

8. See Anderson, *Essays on Roman Satire,* pp. 30–32.

9. See Steiger, p. 338; Maresca, p. 41; Howard Erskine-Hill, *The Augustan Idea,* p. 298.

10. Weinbrot, *Alexander Pope and the Traditions of Formal Verse Satire* (Princeton: Princeton University Press, 1982), p. 213.

11. G. K. Hunter, "The 'Romanticism' of Pope's Horace," in *Essential Articles for the Study of Alexander Pope,* ed. Maynard Mack, rev. and enl. ed. (Hamden, Conn.: Archon Books, 1968), p. 600.

12. One should not, however, overstate the contrast between Pope's and Lucilius's diversions; the latter are not mere "childish relaxations" (Weinbrot, *Alexander Pope,* p. 223), but the relaxations of wise and virtuous men: "*Virtus Scipiadae,* & mitis *Sapientia Laeli*" (72).

13. On Pope's possibly adopting the tones of Persius and Juvenal, see Erskine-Hill, p. 295.

14. Dustin H. Griffin, *Alexander Pope: The Poet in the Poems* (Princeton: Princeton University Press, 1978), p. 189; G. F. C. Plowden, *Pope on Classic Ground* (Athens, Ohio: Ohio University Press, 1983), p. 99.

15. On the poem's ending, cf. Thomas R. Edwards, Jr., who considers the ending a "wry joke" (*This Dark Estate: A Reading of Pope* [Berkeley and Los Angeles: University of California Press, 1963], p. 83). This interpretation is more probable than that of Cedric D. Reverand II, who finds Pope finally triumphing over Fortescue (and his conciliatory advice) in the conclusion to a poem that is "a satirist's forceful, resolute, and convincing proclamation against a corrupt establishment" ("*Ut pictura poesis,* and Pope's 'Satire II, i,'" *Eighteenth-Century Studies* 9 [1976: 556).

Chapter 6. Extremes: Ofellus and the Rake

1. *The Correspondence of Alexander Pope,* ed. George Sherburn, 5 vols. (Oxford: Clarendon Press, 1956), 3:350, 353. See also *Correspondence,* 3:348.

2. See John M. Aden's discussion of the poem, "The Satiric Prolocutor", in *Something like Horace: Studies in the Art and Allusion of Pope's Horatian Satires* (Kingsport, Tenn.: Vanderbilt University Press, 1969), pp. 27–46.

3. I am using the line numbers conforming to Pope's version of the Horatian text, which omits approximately twenty lines.

4 Aden, p. 29.

5. Ibid., pp. 38–42; cf. Weinbrot, *Alexander Pope and the Traditions of Formal Verse Satire* (Princeton: Princeton University Press, 1982), p. 280: ". . . the poem abounds with unfriendly references to Sir Robert and the Hanoverian court."

6. See Aden, pp. 33–34, 42; Howard Erskine-Hill, *The Social Milieu of Alexander Pope: Lives, Example and the Poetic Response* (New Haven: Yale University Press, 1975), pp. 312–13.

7. Cf. Harold Weber's suggestion that "Pope must cling to his separateness" in the *Imitations* because of "his almost obsessive fear that he is about to betray himself" ("The Comic and Tragic Satirist in Pope's *Imitations of Horace,*" *Papers in Language and Literature* 16 [1980]: 75).

8. The quotation is from Frank Stack, *Pope and Horace: Studies in Imitation* (Cambridge: Cambridge University Press, 1985), p. 72. Cf. Maynard Mack, who refers to the poem's "mood of serene urbanity," but speculates that here "Pope sublimates what must have been, in fact, a very keen sense of [his] uncertainties and perils" (*Alexander Pope: A Life* [New York: W. W. Norton, 1985], p. 593). Comparison with the Latin reveals Pope's "sense."

9. Erskine-Hill, p. 316.

10. I question Aden's argument that through *not* including anything equivalent to Horace's lines centering on the "*novus Incola*" (108), the new owner of Ofellus's farm, Pope intended "a devastating allusion to George II, Hanoverian England, and the perversion of *dominium*" (p. 45).

11. Erskine-Hill, p. 316.

12. Weinbrot, *Alexander Pope,* p. 280.

13. G. Douglas Atkins, "Strategy and Purpose in Pope's *Sober Advice from Horace,*" *Papers in Language and Literature* 15 (1979): 161, 160.

14. Ibid., p. 165. Referring to this "gallery of satiric portraits," Aden con-

vincingly claims that Pope "commences the Imitation in the spirit and manner of *To a Lady*" (p. 58).

15. Geoffrey Tillotson, *Pope and Human Nature* (Oxford: Clarendon Press, 1958), p. 117.

16. Brower, *Alexander Pope: The Poetry of Allusion* (Oxford: Clarendon Press, 1959), p. 293.

17. For the identities of the dean and lords, see Butt's notes to these line. Line 43 is puzzling: why should Pope either hint or risk being understood as hinting at his being homosexual, especially since he sneers at Hervey as homosexual in line 92? In the *Epistle to Augustus,* line 236, "sings down Pope and Turk," certainly refers to Pope; see chapter 8. Possibly he was thinking of Horace's 116–18, although his rendering of these lines does not refer to homosexuality.

18. Cf. Atkins on the allusion to Paul (p. 166).

19. Ibid., p. 165.

20. "Stupendous whole" is, of course, from the *Essay on Man:* Epistle 1, line 267. On the connection in thought between *Sober Advice* and both the *Essay on Man* and the *Epistles to Several Persons,* see Aden, p. 55; cf. Stack's ill-advised judgment that Pope's lines 96–105 are "a parody of his own moral thinking in the *Paraphrase of Satire II.ii.* and the *Essay on Man*" (p. 89).

Chapter 7. Refuge in a Toppling World

1. Reuben Arthur Brower, *Alexander Pope: The Poetry of Allusion* (Oxford: Clarendon Press, 1959), p. 294.

2. On the possible allusion to Juvenal's patron, see Weinbrot, *Alexander Pope and the Traditions of Formal Verse Satire* (Princeton: Princeton University Press, 1982), p. 254.

3. Erskine-Hill, *Augustan Idea,* p. 312.

4. Some additional lines from the third satire's portrait of Tigellius will give an idea of how "seesaw" was his wit:

> Often he ran as if pursued
> by enemies, more often marched like a maiden bearer
> of Juno's sacred gifts. Sometimes he owned two hundred slaves,
> sometimes ten. One moment he'd babble about kings and despots,
> the next he'd say, "Just give me a three-legged table,
> a plain shaker for unscented salt, and any rag of a toga
> to keep me warm."
>
> (9–15)

Compare the portrait of Sporus.

5. Thomas R. Edwards. Jr., *This Dark Estate: A Reading of Pope* (Berkeley and California: University of California Press, 1963), p. 104; Dustin H. Griffin, *Alexander Pope: The Poet in the Poems* (Princeton: Princeton University Press, 1978), p. 199.

6. See *Sat.* 1.4.105–26 on this "best of fathers" who "taught me how to live" (105–6).

7. Aubrey L. Williams, "*Pope and Horace:* The Second Epistle of the Second Book," in *Restoration and Eighteenth-Century Literature,* ed. Carroll Camden (Chicago: University of Chicago Press, 1963), p. 321; Fredric V. Bogel, *Acts of Knowledge: Pope's Later Poems* (Lewisburg, Pa.: Bucknell University Press,

1981), p. 129; Thomas E. Maresca, *Pope's Horatian Poems* (Columbus: Ohio State University Press, 1966), p. 147. Cf. the more accurate interpretation of Frank Stack: Pope "appears very confident" in lines 284–303, but the very last lines (304–27) contain "the feeling of age, of potential bitterness, and of continued emotional strain" (*Pope and Horace: Studies in Imitation* [Cambridge: Cambridge University Press, 1985] pp. 147–48).

8. Williams, p. 313; see also Maresca, p. 119.

9. Bogel, p. 116.

10. See Eduard Fraenkel (from whom I quote), *Horace* (Oxford: Clarendon Press, 1957), p. 308.

11. C. W. Macleod, "The Poetry of Ethics: Horace, *Epistles* I," *Journal of Roman Studies* 69 (1979): 19.

12. Bogel, pp. 117, 120.

13. See "The Roman Socrates: Horace and his Satires," in Anderson's *Essays on Roman Satire* (Princeton: Princeton University Press, 1982), pp. 13–49.

14. Stack, p. 137.

15. Weinbrot, *Alexander Pope*, pp. 284, 285.

Chapter 8. Confronting the Age

1. *Augustus Caesar in "Augustan" England*, pp. x, 192.

2. See Weinbrot on the poem (*AC*, pp. 182–217). This interpretation, we are told in the preface to his book, "should serve as a test case for the practical value of the historical reclamation [i.e., the argument that the eighteenth century was really anti-Augustan] in earlier chapters" (p. x). Note that Weinbrot does not claim that his study of the *Augustus* will validate the "reclamation" itself; he assumes its validity when discussing the poem. The meaning of "practical value" is not clear to me.

3. Cf. Erskine-Hill on Pope's use of Augustus as a "positive example" (*Augustan Idea*, p. 326).

4. Ibid., p. 330.

5. Although Eduard Fraenkel discerns more than five parts in *Epist.* 2.1, my way of dividing the poem is based on his. My general debt in this chapter to Fraenkel will be apparent. See chapter 8, "The Letter to Augustus," of his *Horace* (Oxford: Clarendon Press, 1957), pp. 383–99.

6. See Fraenkel on the *"laudes Caesaris"* in lines 1–17 (p. 386) and on "Roman poetry and Augustus" as Horace's "principal theme" after line 214 (p. 394).

7. Horace refers specifically to Livius Andronicus, but it is obvious that Livius stands for all of the older Latin poets.

8. Fraenkel, pp. 388–90. He sums up: "what [Horace] wants to provide and does provide is a pair of sharply contrasted pictures, which, as he goes on, are to merge into a harmonious complex" (pp. 389–90).

9. The lines numbered 120 and 125 in the Twickenham Edition's Horatian text are actually 119 and 124. To avoid confusion, I will use the correct line numbers in referring to this passage.

10. In a footnote to his own line 204, Pope says that Horace's *"Os tenerum pueri,* is ridicule." However, "the nobler office of a Poet follows, *Torquet ab obscoenis. . . ."*

11. Fraenkel (p. 391) suggests the intended allusion to the *Aeneid;* Suetonius's life of Horace mentions Augustus's request for this epistle.

12. Frank Stack, *Pope and Horace: Studies in Imitation* (Cambridge: Cambridge University Press, 1985), p. 175.

13. Fraenkel, p. 391.

14. Ibid., p. 392.

15. "My name is as bad a one as yours, and hated by all bad poets, from Hopkins and Sternhold to Gilden and Cibber. The first prayed against me joined with the Turk . . ." (Pope to Swift, 15 October 1725). Quoted by Butt, p. 215. See Maynard Mack on Pope's low opinion of Sternhold (*Alexander Pope: A Life* [New York: W. W. Norton, 1985], p. 298).

16. On this "recusatio," see Fraenkel, pp. 397–98.

Chapter 9. Toward Silence

1. John M. Aden, *Something like Horace: Studies in the Art and Allusion of Pope's Horatian Satires* (Kingsport, Tenn.: Vanderbilt University Press, 1969), p. 83.

2. On Pope's appeal to Murray, see Aden, pp. 69–73; Erskine-Hill, *Augustan Idea*, p. 334; Frank Stack, *Pope and Horace: Studies in Imitation* (Cambridge: Cambridge University Press, 1985), p. 206.

3. Weinbrot, *Alexander Pope and the Traditions of Formal Verse Satire* (Princeton: Princeton University Press, 1982), p. 291; Fredric V. Bogel, *Acts of Knowledge: Pope's Later Poems* (Lewisburg, Pa.: Bucknell University Press, 1981), p. 134.

4. Aden (citing Tupper), p. 72; Sellar, *The Roman Poets of the Augustan Age: Horace and the Elegiac Poets* (Oxford: Clarendon Press, 1899), p. 95.

5. "A Letter from Artemisia in the Town to Chloe in the Country," lines 44, 33, 51 (in *The Complete Poems of John Wilmot, Earl of Rochester,* ed. David M. Vieth [New Haven: Yale University Press, 1968]).

6. Bogel, pp. 134, 136.

7. Compare the ambivalence H. T. Dickinson notes in Bolingbroke in the late 1730s toward "a new generation of politicians" who might be roused against Walpole. Bolingbroke attempted "moral exhortation," but "in his heart he must have known that the situation would not be changed by a few young patriots" (*Bolingbroke* [London: Constable & Company, 1970], pp. 256, 257).

8. See Bertram A. Goldgar, *Walpole and the Wits: The Relation of Politics to Literature, 1722–1742* (Lincoln, Nebr.: University of Nebraska Press, 1976), p. 166; Erskine-Hill, p. 339.

9. Perhaps Pope omitted the conventional lines 49–51 from his Horatian text because they contain another vulgar comparison: the aspiring philosopher is likened to a "small-time wrestler" hoping to win a championship.

10. See Eduard Fraenkel, *Horace* (Oxford: Clarendon Press, 1957), p. 308.

11. Mack, *The Garden and the City: Retirement and Politics in the Later Poetry of Pope 1731–1743* (Toronto: University of Toronto Press, 1969), pp. 137, 131–32.

12. Cf. Bogel on the "parenthetical remarks": "their very placement mimics a reluctance to claim as much as is claimed by the ends of the clauses they interrupt" (p. 149).

13. Compare Horace's matter-of-factness: " "Ne cures ea que *stulte* miraris & optas / Discere, & audire, & meliori credere non vis?" (47–48) ("To stop caring about these things you gawk at and desire, / can't you listen to, learn from, and believe a wiser man?").

14. Stack, p. 265. Stack also notes that Pope appears to adopt Horace's tone in the imitation's lines 134–60.

15. For Bolingbroke's somewhat fulsome praise of retirement, see his letter to

Swift, 20 March 1731 (*The Correspondence of Alexander Pope,* ed. George Sherburne, 5 vols. [Oxford: Clarendon Press, 1956], 3:184); Dickinson, p. 249.

16. *Correspondence,* 4:45, 50.

17. Stack, p. 272.

18. See Northrop Frye's discussion, "The Mythos of Spring: Comedy," in his *Anatomy of Criticism: Four Essays* (Princeton: Princeton University Press, 1957), pp. 163–86. On comedy's final union, see pp. 163–64.

19. For quotations, see Frye, p. 163.

20. Ibid., p. 169.

21. Ibid., p. 165.

22. Goldgar, pp. 167–68.

Appendix

1. Erskine-Hill, *Augustan Idea,* p. 345.

2. Line 8 of Dialogue 1 closely paraphrases line 68 of the imitation of *Sat.* 2.1: "While Tories call me Whig, and Whigs a Tory." The "source" for this is the Latin line 34: Horace, whose birthplace is Venusia, is "unsure if I'm Lucanian or Apulian" because "Venusia's farmers plow along both borders" (35). Line 10 of Dialogue 1 similarly paraphrases the imitation's line 40: "And laugh at Peers that put their Trust in *Peter.*" This and the preceding three lines are parallel to Horace's 21–23, which say nothing about noblemen and their moneylender. Trebatius advises against

> . . . wounding with your surly lines
> Pantolabus the leech, Nomentanus the spendthrift,
> for all fear you, even those untouched, and hate you.

Select Bibliography

Addison, Joseph, *Poems on Several Occasions with a Dissertation upon the Roman Poets.* London, 1719.

———. *Dialogues upon the Usefulness of Ancient Medals.* Vol. 2 of *The Miscellaneous Works of Joseph Addison.* Edited by A. C. Guthkelch. London: G. Bell and Sons, 1914.

Aden, John M. *Something like Horace: Studies in the Art and Allusion of Pope's Horatian Satires.* Kingsport, Tenn.: Vanderbilt University Press, 1969.

Anderson, William S. *Essays on Roman Satire.* Princeton: Princeton University Press, 1982.

———. "Ironic Preambles and Satiric Self-Definition in Horace *Satire* 2.1." *Pacific Coast Philology* 19 (1984): 35–42.

Atkins, G. Douglas. "Strategy and Purpose in Pope's *Sober Advice from Horace.*" *Papers in Language and Literature* 15 (1979): 159–74.

Bentley, Richard. *Q. Horatius Flaccus ex Recensione & cum Notis atque Emendationibus.* Cambridge, 1711.

Blackwell, Thomas. *Memoirs of the Court of Augustus.* 3 vols. Edinburgh, 1753–63.

Bloom, Edward A., and Lillian D. Bloom. "Johnson's *London* and Its Juvenalian Texts." *Huntington Library Quarterly* 34 (1970): 1–23.

———. "Johnson's *London* and the Tools of Scholarship." *Huntington Library Quarterly* 34 (1971): 115–39.

Bogel, Fredric V. *Acts of Knowledge: Pope's Later Poems.* Lewisburg, Pa.: Bucknell University Press, 1981.

Bolingbroke, Henry St. John. *The Works of the Late Honorable Henry St. John, Lord Viscount Bolingbroke.* Edited by David Mallet. 5 vols. 1754. Reprint. Hildesheim, West Germany: Georg Olms, 1968.

———. *Historical Writings by Lord Bolingbroke.* Edited by Isaac Kramnick. Chicago: University of Chicago Press, 1972.

Boyle, John. *The First Ode of the First Book of Horace Imitated.* London, 1741.

Brooks, Harold F. "The 'Imitation' in English Poetry, Especially in Formal Satire, before the Age of Pope." *Review of English Studies* 25 (1949): 124–40.

Brower, Reuben Arthur. *Alexander Pope: The Poetry of Allusion.* Oxford: Clarendon Press, 1959.

Brown, John. *An Essay on Satire Occasioned by the Death of Mr. Pope.* London, 1745.

Butt, John. "Johnson's Practice in the Poetical Imitation." In *New Light on Dr. Johnson: Essays on the Occasion of His 250th Birthday,* edited by Frederick W. Hilles, pp. 19–34. New Haven: Yale University Press, 1959.

Carnochan, W. B. *Lemuel Gulliver's Mirror for Man*. Berkeley and Los Angeles: University of California Press, 1968.

Carretta, Vincent. *The Snarling Muse: Verbal and Visual Political Satire from Pope to Churchill*. Philadelphia: University of Pennsylvania Press, 1983.

Catrou, [François], and [Pierre] Rouillé. *The Roman History, with Notes Historical, Geographical, and Critical*. Translated by R. Bundy. 6 vols. London, 1728–37.

Clarke, John. *An Introduction to the Making of Latin*. 1721. Reprint. Menston, England: Scolar Press, 1970.

Crusius, Lewis. *The Lives of the Roman Poets*. 3rd ed. 2 vols. London, 1753.

Davis, Herbert. "The Augustan Conception of History." In *Reason and the Imagination: Studies in the History of Ideas, 1600–1800*, edited by J. A. Mazzeo, pp. 213–29. New York: Columbia University Press, 1962.

Denham, John. Preface to *The Destruction of Troy*. In *The Poetical Works of Sir John Denham*, edited by Theodore Howard Banks. New Haven: Yale University Press, 1928.

Dennis, John. *The Critical Works of John Dennis*. Edited by Edward Niles Hooker. 2 vols. Baltimore: Johns Hopkins University Press, 1939 and 1943.

Dickinson, H. T. *Bolingbroke*. London: Constable and Company, 1970.

———. *Liberty and Property: Political Ideology in Eighteenth-Century Britain*. New York: Holmes and Meier, 1977.

Dryden, John. *Essays of John Dryden*. Edited by W. P. Ker. 2 vols. New York: Russell and Russell, 1961.

Edwards, Thomas R., Jr. *This Dark Estate: A Reading of Pope*. Berkeley and Los Angeles: University of California Press, 1963.

Ehrenpreis, Irvin. *Literary Meaning and Augustan Values*. Charlottesville, Va.: University Press of Virginia, 1974.

Eliade, Mircea. *Cosmos and History: The Myth of the Eternal Return*. New York: Harper and Row, 1959.

Erskine-Hill, Howard. "Augustans on Augustanism: England, 1655–1759." *Renaissance and Modern Studies* 11 (1967): 55–83.

———. *The Social Milieu of Alexander Pope: Lives, Example and the Poetic Response*. New Haven: Yale University Press, 1975.

———. *The Augustan Idea in English Literature*. London: Edward Arnold, 1983.

Fraenkel, Eduard. *Horace*. Oxford: Clarendon Press, 1957.

Frye, Northrop. *The Anatomy of Criticism: Four Essays*. Princeton: Princeton University Press, 1957.

Fuchs, Jacob. "Women, 'Learned Lumber,' and English Neoclassical Poetry." *Pacific Coast Philology* 15 (1980): 27–34.

Goad, Carolyn. *Horace in the English Literature of the Eighteenth Century*. New Haven: Yale University Press, 1918.

Goldgar, Bertrand A. *Walpole and the Wits: The Relation of Politics to Literature, 1722–1742*. Lincoln, Nebr.: University of Nebraska Press, 1976.

Goldsmith, Oliver. *The History of Rome from the Foundation of the City of Rome to the Destruction of the Eastern Empire*. 2 vols. London, 1827.

Griffin, Dustin H. *Alexander Pope: The Poet in the Poems*. Princeton: Princeton University Press, 1978.

Harte, Walter. *An Essay on Satire*. 1730. Reprint. Los Angeles: Augustan Reprint Society, 1968.

Hirsch, E. D., Jr. *Validity in Interpretation*. New Haven: Yale University Press, 1967.

———. "Meaning and Significance Reinterpreted." *Critical Inquiry* 11 (1984): 202–25.

Hooke, Nathaniel. *The Roman History, from the Building of Rome to the Ruin of the Commonwealth*. 4th ed. 11 vols. London, 1766–71.

Horace. *The Odes and Epodes of Horace*. Translated by Joseph P. Clancy. Chicago: University of Chicago Press, 1960.

———. *Horace's Satires and Epistles*. Translated by Jacob Fuchs. New York: W. W. Norton, 1977.

Hughes, R. E. "Pope's *Imitations of Horace* and the Ethical Focus." *Modern Language Notes* 71 (1956): 569–74.

Hunter, G. K. "The 'Romanticism' of Pope's Horace." In *Essential Articles for the Study of Alexander Pope*, rev. and enl. ed., edited by Maynard Mack, pp. 591–606. Hamden, Conn.: Archon, 1968.

Hurd, Richard. *Q. Horatii Flacci, Epistolae ad Pisones et Augustum with an English Commentary and Notes*. 5th ed. 2 vols. London, 1776.

Iser, Wolfgang. "Indeterminacy and the Reader's Response in Prose Fiction." In *Aspects of Narrative: Selected Papers from the English Institute,* edited by J. Hillis Miller, pp. 1–45. New York: Columbia University Press, 1971.

———. "The Reading Process: A Phenomenological Approach." *New Literary History* 3 (1972): 279–99.

———. *The Act of Reading: A Theory of Aesthetic Response*. Baltimore: Johns Hopkins University Press, 1978.

Johnson, James William. "The Meaning of 'Augustan.' " *Journal of the History of Ideas* 19 (1958): 507–22.

———. *The Formation of English Neo-Classical Thought*. Princeton: Princeton University Press, 1967.

Johnson, Samuel. *Lives of the English Poets*. Edited by George Birbeck Hill. 3 vols. Oxford: Clarendon Press, 1905.

———. *The Rambler*. Edited by W. J. Bate and Albrecht B. Strauss. Vol. 5 of *The Yale Edition of the Works of Samuel Johnson*. New Haven: Yale University Press, 1969.

———. *The Poems of Samuel Johnson*. 2nd ed. Edited by David Nichol Smith and Edward L. McAdam. Oxford: Clarendon Press, 1974.

Juvenal. *Juvenal and Persius*. Translated by G. G. Ramsey. Loeb Classical Library. New York: G. P. Putnam's Sons, 1918.

Kelsall, Malcolm. "What God, What Mortal? The *Aeneid* and English Mock-Heroic." *Arion* 8 (1969): 359–79.

———. "Augustus and Pope." *Huntington Library Quarterly* 39 (1976): 117–31.

Kupersmith, William. "Vice and Folly in Neoclassical Satire." *Genre* 11 (1978): 45–62.

Lascelles, Mary. "Johnson and Juvenal." In *New Light on Dr. Johnson: Essays on the Occasion of his 250th Birthday,* edited by Frederick W. Hilles, pp. 35–55. New Haven: Yale University Press, 1959.

Le Moine d'Orgival. *Considerations sur l'Origine et le Progrès des Belles Lettres chez les Romains et les Causes de Leur Decadence*. Amsterdam, 1750.

Levine, Jay Arnold. "Pope's *Epistle to Augustus*, Lines 1–30." *Studies in English Literature, 1500–1900* 7 (1967): 427–51.

Lyttelton, George. *Dialogues of the Dead*. London, 1760.

Mack, Maynard. *The Garden and the City: Retirement and Politics in the Later Poetry of Pope 1731–1743*. Toronto: University of Toronto Press, 1969.

————. *Alexander Pope: A Life*. New York: W. W. Norton, 1985.

Macleod, C. W. "The Poetry of Ethics: Horace, *Epistles* I." *Journal of Roman Studies* 69 (1979): 16–27.

Maidwell, Lewis. *An Essay upon the Necessity and Excellency of Education*. 1705. Reprint. Los Angeles: Augustan Reprint Society, 1955.

Maresca, Thomas E. *Pope's Horatian Poems*. Columbus: Ohio State University Press, 1966.

Montagu, Mary Wortley. *Essays and Poems and Simplicity, A Comedy*. Edited by Robert Halsband and Isobel Grundy. Oxford: Clarendon Press, 1977.

Morris, Edward P., ed. *Horace: Satires and Epistles*. 1939. Reprint. Norman, Okla.: University of Oklahoma Press, 1968.

Nadel, George H. "Philosophy of History before Historicism." *History and Theory* 3 (1964): 291–315.

Paulson, Ronald. "Satire, and Poetry, and Pope." In *English Satire: Papers Read at a Clark Library Seminar, January 15, 1972*, pp. 57–106. Los Angeles: William Andrews Clark Memorial Library, 1972.

Pierce, Charles E., Jr. *The Religious Life of Samuel Johnson*. Hamden, Conn.: Archon Books, 1983.

Plowden, G. F. C. *Pope on Classic Ground*. Athens, Ohio: Ohio University Press, 1983.

Pope, Alexander. *The Twickenham Edition of the Poems of Alexander Pope*. Edited by John Butt et al. 11 vols. New Haven: Yale University Press, 1939–1969.

————. *The Correspondence of Alexander Pope*. Edited by George Sherburn. 5 vols. Oxford: Clarendon Press, 1956.

Preston, Thomas R. "Historiography as Art in Eighteenth-Century England." *Texas Studies in Literature and Language* 11 (1969): 1209–21.

Prior, Matthew. *The Literary Works of Matthew Prior*. Edited by H. Bunker Wright and Monroe K. Spears. 2 vols. Oxford: Clarendon Press, 1959.

Rand, Edward Kennard. *The Building of Eternal Rome*. Cambridge, Mass.: Harvard University Press, 1943.

Reverand, Cedric D., II. "*Ut pictura poesis* and Pope's 'Satire II, i.'" *Eighteenth-Century Studies* 9 (1976): 553–68.

Rollin, [Charles]. *The History of the Arts and Sciences of the Antients*. Translated by John Stacie. 4 vols. London, 1739.

Rollin, [Charles], and [Jean Baptiste Louis] Crévier. *The Roman History from the Foundation of Rome to the Battle of Actium*. Translator anon. 16 vols. London, 1739–47.

Rudd, Niall. *The Satires of Horace*. Cambridge: Cambridge University Press, 1966.

Selden, R. "Dr. Johnson and Juvenal: A Problem in Critical Method." *Comparative Literature* 22 (1970): 289–302.

Sellar, W. Y. *The Roman Poets of the Augustan Age: Horace and the Elegiac Poets.* Oxford: Clarendon Press, 1892.

Spence, Joseph. *Polymetis: or an Enquiry concerning the Agreement between the Works of the Roman Poets, and the Remains of the Antient Artists.* London, 1747.

———. *Observations, Anecdotes, and Characters of Books and Men.* Edited by James M. Osborn. 2 vols. Oxford: Clarendon Press, 1966.

Stack, Frank. *Pope and Horace: Studies in Imitation.* Cambridge: Cambridge University Press, 1985.

Steiger, Richard. "Pope's 'Augustan' Horace." *Arethusa* 10 (1977): 321–52.

Steiner, George. *After Babel: Aspects of Language and Translation.* New York and London: Oxford University Press, 1975.

Swift, Jonathan. *A Discourse of the Contests and Dissentions between the Nobles and the Commons in Athens and Rome.* Edited by Frank H. Ellis. Oxford: Clarendon Press, 1967.

Thompson, James Westfall, and Bernard J. Holm. *A History of Historical Writing.* 2 vols. New York: MacMillan, 1942.

Tillotson, Geoffrey. *Pope and Human Nature.* Oxford: Clarendon Press, 1958.

Trapp, Joseph. *The Preface to the Aeneis of Virgil.* 1718. Reprint. Los Angeles: Augustan Reprint Society, 1982.

———. *Lectures on Poetry.* London, 1742.

Tytler, Alexander. *Essay on the Principles of Translation.* London, 1791.

Vergil. *The Aeneid of Virgil.* Translated by Alan Mandelbaum. Berkeley. University of California Press, 1971.

Warton, Joseph. Introduction to *The Works of Virgil in Latin and English.* Translated by Christopher Pitt. 4 vols. London, 1753.

———. *An Essay on the Genius and Writings of Pope.* 2 vols. 1782. Reprint. Farnborough, England: Gregg International, 1969.

Watt, Ian. "Two Historical Aspects of the Augustan Tradition." In *Studies in the Eighteenth Century: Papers Presented at the David Nichol Smith Memorial Seminar, Canberra, 1966,* edited by R. F. Brissenden, pp. 67–79. Toronto: University of Toronto Press, 1966.

Weber, Harold. "The Comic and Tragic Satirist in Pope's *Imitations of Horace.*" *Papers in Language and Literature* 16 (1980): 66–80.

———. "'Comic Humour and Tragic Spirit': The Augustan Distinction between Horace and Juvenal." *Classical and Modern Literature* 1 (1981): 275–89.

Weinbrot, Howard D. "History, Horace, and Augustus Caesar: Some Implications for Eighteenth-Century Satire." *Eighteenth-Century Studies* 7 (1974): 391–414.

———. "Johnson's *London* and Juvenal's Third Satire: The Country as 'Ironic Norm.'" *Modern Philology* 73 (Supplement, 1976): S56–65.

———. *Augustus Caesar in "Augustan" England: The Decline of a Cultural Norm.* Princeton: Princeton University Press, 1978.

———. *Alexander Pope and the Traditions of Formal Verse Satire.* Princeton: Princeton University Press, 1982.

Weinsheimer, Joel. "'London' and the Fundamental Problem of Hermeneutics." *Critical Inquiry* 9 (1982): 303–22.

[Whitehead, Paul?]. *The State of Rome under Nero and Domitian: A Satire*. London, 1739.

Williams, Aubrey L. "*Pope and Horace:* The Second Epistle of the Second Book." In *Restoration and Eighteenth-Century Literature: Essays in Honor of Alan Dugald McKillop,* edited by Carroll Camden, pp. 309–21. Chicago: University of Chicago Press, 1963.

Wilmot, John, Earl of Rochester. *The Complete Poems of John Wilmot, Earl of Rochester.* Edited by David M. Vieth. New Haven: Yale University Press, 1968.

Index

Addison, Joseph, 46, 118
Aden, John, 78, 124, 125, 154n.10, 154–55n.14
Aeneid (Vergil), 54, 56, 118, 150n.12
Anderson, William S., 104, 153n.4
Application of source meaning, 26, 147n.20; strained, 15–16, 20, 22–23, 61–62, 65, 71, 78, 82
Arbuthnot, John, 43. See also *Epistle to Dr. Arbuthnot*
Ars Poetica (Horace), 15
Atkins, G. Douglas, 85, 90
Augustan Age, 78, 85, 95–96; culture in, 76, 118–20; eighteenth-century attitude to, 21–22, 28–30
Augustus Caesar: compared with George II, 31–35, 75, 149n.14; as despot, 30–33; eighteenth-century reputation of, 21–22, 28–41, 52, 112–14, 148n.3; as exemplar, 29, 33, 135, 156n.3; and Horace, 42–46, 70, 101; Horace on, 21–22, 51, 54, 58–59, 65, 136; opposition journalism and, 33–38; Pope's conception of, 37

Bentley, Richard, 45
Blackmore, Richard, 74, 102, 119
Blackwell, Thomas, 44
Bloom, Edward A., and Lillian D., 146n.3
Bogel, Fredric V., 60, 100, 104, 128, 157n.12
Boileau-Despréaux, Nicolas, 48, 69, 71, 151n.24
Bolingbroke, Henry St. John, 34, 63, 70–74, 81, 96, 128–29, 137–42, 149n.20, 157n.7, 157–58n.15; on Augustus, 31–32, 35, 38, 41
Boyle, John, 16, 19
Brooks, Harold F., 17
Brower, Reuben Arthur, 42
Brown, John, 47–48
Butt, John, 22, 82, 96, 144

Carmen Saeculare (Horace), 118–21
Caroline, Queen, 95, 99
Carretta, Vincent, 149n.15
Cato, Marcus Porcius, 39–41
Catullus (Domitian's minister), 20
Censorship, press, 36–37
Charles II, 32
Chartres, Francis, 74, 124
Cibber, Colley, 75, 118, 119, 157n.15
Cicero, 39
Clarke, John, 148n.8
Classics, 94; education in, 53
"Compartmentalized response," 38–41
Corneille, Pierre, 116
Craftsman, 33–37, 48–51, 149n.18
Crusius, Lewis, 44–47, 54, 150–51n.15

Denham, John, 17
Dennis, John, 46
Dialogues of the Dead (Lyttelton), 39–41, 45–46, 48
Dickinson, H. T., 140, 149n.20, 157n.7
Domitian, 20, 51–51
Dryden, John, 43–44, 46–47, 75, 96, 146n.5, 149n.14; Pope on, 63, 68–69, 71
Dunciad, The (Pope), 54, 92, 124, 142

Edwards, Thomas R., Jr., 152nn. 11 and 12, 154n.15
Eliade, Mircea, 32
Epilogue to the Satires (Pope), 60–61, 124, 143–45
Epist. 1.1 (Horace), 58, 129–42
Epist. 1.6 (Horace), 124–28
Epist. 1.7 (Horace), 45
Epist., 1.8 (Horace), 44
Epist. 1.11 (Horace), 55
Epist. 1.12 (Horace), 55
Epist. 1.17 (Horace), 49
Epist. 2.1 (Horace), 29, 44, 112–23, 156n.5
Epist. 2.2 (Horace), 97–111

Epistle to Augustus (Pope), 29, 33, 44, 111, 112–23, 155 n.17; art in, 116–18, 121; irony in, 113–14, 122

Epistle to Bathurst (Pope), 77, 136

Epistle to Burlington (Pope), 63

Epistle to Dr. Arbuthnot, An (Pope), 63, 75, 93–97, 102, 110, 121, 123, 144

Erskine-Hill, Howard, 29–30, 32, 38, 43, 62, 81–82, 113, 129, 149 n.14, 156 n.3

Essay on Criticism, An (Pope), 110

Essay on Man, An (Pope), 120, 155 n.20

Examples in literature, 58–59

First Epistle of the First Book of Horace Imitated, The (Pope), 128–42; retirement in, 134, 137, 140–42; satire in, 131–34, 137, 139, 142

First Epistle of the Second Book of Horace, Imitated, The (Pope). See *Epistle to Augustus*

First Ode of the First Book of Horace Imitated, The (Boyle), 19–20

First Satire of the Second Book of Horace Imitated, The (Pope), 63–76, 95

Florus, Julius, 97, 99–100

Fortescue, William, 65, 73–75, 122–24

Fraenkel, Eduard, 116, 156 nn. 5, 8, and 11

Frye, Northrop, 141

Gadamer, Hans-Georg, 26

Gaps. See Imitation: gaps in

Gay, John, 32, 95

George I, 118, 148 n.3

George II, 50; compared with Augustus, 31–35, 75, 101, 112–13, 148 n.3; and Pope, 61, 71, 74–75; Pope on, 59, 95, 99, 101, 118, 121–22, 131–35, 141, 149–50 n.21

Gilmore, Thomas B., 151 n.24

Goad, Carolyn, 53

Goldgar, Bertrand A., 50, 149 n.15, 157 n.8

Gordon, Thomas, 35, 36

Griffin, Dustin H., 73

Harte, Walter, 48

Henley the Orator, 49

Hervey, John, 63, 74

Hirsch, E. D., Jr., 21, 26, 58, 147 n.20

Historical cycles, 32–33, 149 n.10

Homer: Pope's translation of, 17

Hooke, Nathaniel, 30–31, 38–39, 41

Hopkins, John, 120–21, 157 n.15

Horace: on Augustus, 112–14, 123, 134; compared with Pope, 16, 65, 68–76, 77–78; eighteenth-century reputation of, 21, 28–29, 38, 42–52; friends of, 45, 70–72, 96–97, 150–51 n.15 (*see also* Maecenas); imitations of, 15–16, 19 (see also *Imitations of Horace* [Pope]); as imperial poet, 45, 53–59, 101, 110, 113, 118–19; and Juvenal, 46–51; life of, 56, 158 n.2; on nature, 90–92; patrons of, 95–96, 137–38 (*see also* Maecenas); as political exemplar, 48–52; realism of, 54; and retirement, 96, 102–3, 130–31, 142; as satirist, 43, 46–49, 64, 68–69, 122, 136, 139, 151 n.24; *sermones* by, 54–55, 126; style of, 70–71, 126, 157 n.13. *See also* individual poems

"Horace, Satyr 4. Lib. 1. Paraphrased" (Pope), 63

Hughes, R. E., 146 n.2

Hunter, G. K., 68

Hurd, Richard, 43–44

Imitation: gaps in, 17–21, 65, 144; reading of, 15–27; and sources, 15–17, 26; and translation, 16–18

Imitations of Horace (Pope): contrast of, to sources, 59–61; patronage in, 74–76, 94–96; writing of, 29, 33, 63. *See also* individual poems

Iser, Wolfgang, 18–19, 21, 146 n.8

Johnson, James William, 28, 148 n.3

Johnson, Samuel: on historical cycles, 149 n.10; on imitation, 15–16, 62; imitations by, 22–27, 146 n.3

Juvenal: compared with Horace, 46–51, 151 n.19; in *Imitations of Horace,* 62, 70–71; Johnson's imitations of, 22–27; Prior's imitation of, 21; seventh satire of, 21, 93; tenth satire of, 22–26; third satire of, 22, 26–27; Whitehead's imitation of, 20

Kelsall, Malcolm, 148 n.1

Kupersmith, William, 151 n.25

Laelius, 69, 70–71
Land: ownership of, 82–84, 104–6
Le Moine d'Orgival, 45–46
Lesser and greater order, 73
Levine, Jay Arnold, 38
Lex majestatis, 34–37
Livius Andronicus, 156 n.7
London (Johnson), 22, 26
Lucilius, 63, 65–74, 78, 153 n.12
Lyttelton, George, 39–41, 45–46, 48, 150 nn. 12 and 13

Mack, Maynard, 131, 149 n.15, 154 n.8, 157 n.15
Macleod, C. W., 103
Maecenas, 43, 45–46, 93, 95, 129; as friend of Horace, 46, 56–59, 70; as patron, 37–38, 101, 137–38, 141–42
Maidwell, Lewis, 45
Maresca, Thomas E., 146 n.3, 153 n.7
Messalla Corvinus, 39–41
Mimnermus, 127
Montagu, Lady Mary Wortley, 45
Montagu, Wortley, 106
Morris, Edward P., 64
Murray, William, 125–28

New Dunciad (Pope), 124

Octavian. *See* Augustus Caesar
Odes (Horace), 44, 51, 130
Ofellus, 77–85, 90, 106

Pastorals (Pope), 54
Patronage, literary, 94–96, 112–13, 119, 138
Paulson, Ronald, 152 n.6
Persius, 46–47, 62, 70–71
Peterborough, third earl of, 70–71, 73, 81
Philosophy: Pope and Horace on, 102–4, 129–31, 139
Plowden, G. F. C., 73
Pope, Alexander: and Augustus, 37, 113, 141, 156 n.3; and Bolingbroke, 63, 70–74, 128–29, 137–42; contrasted with Horace, 60–62, 65, 68–70, 77, 86–87, 97–98, 106–11, 113, 128, 141; cynicism of, 127, 135; and Dryden, 68; early poetry of, 152 n.6; education of, 53, 97–98; as exemplar, 67; friends of, 70–72, 82, 96–97 (*see*

also Bolingbroke, Henry St. John); and George II, 61, 74–76, 101, 118, 121–22, 130–35, 141; home of, *see* Twickenham; on Horace, 42–43, 143–44; and Horace's Ofellus, 78–80; as imitator of Horace, 65, 146 n.3 (*see also* individual poems); isolation of, 59, 68–70, 96–97, 124; and Juvenal, 62, 93; on nature, 90–92; as opposition poet, 33, 113; retirement of, 101–4, 129–31, 134, 136–37, 140–42; as satirist, 61–63, 73–74, 125, 129, 137; and Vergil, 42–43, 54; on writing, 109–10, 119, 131
Prior, Matthew, 21

Racine, Jean, 116
Rand, E. K., 54
Rape of the Lock, The, (Pope), 54
Retirement, 96, 157–58 n.15. See also Pope, Alexander: retirement of; Horace: and retirement
Reverand, Cedric D., II, 154 n.15
Rollin, Charles, 45, 150–51 n.15
Rome: Augustan, 28, 31, 45–46, 54–57, 72, 76, 95–96; contrasted with England, 60–61, 110–11, 116, 124; Horace on, 101–2, 116–20, 134, 142
Rudd, Niall, 64

Sat. 1.2 (Horace), 85–93
Sat. 1.3 (Horace), 93, 155 n.4
Sat. 1.4 (Horace): imitation of, 63–64, 66–67
Sat. 1.6 (Horace), 45
Sat. 1.10 (Horace), 66–67
Sat. 2.1 (Horace), 37, 63–76
Sat. 2.2 (Horace), 77–85, 106
Sat. 2.3 (Horace), 37, 49
Sat. 2.6 (Horace), 56–58, 60
Sat. 2.8 (Horace), 93
Satire, 119, 142, 144; effectiveness of, 62, 66–67, 73–76, 85, 92, 122, 125, 128–33; Horatian, 47–48, 92; and philosophy, 133–37; political, 151 n.25
"Satyr on the Poets" (Prior), 21
Scipio Africanus, 65, 69, 70, 71
Second Epistle of the Second Book of Horace, Imitated, The (Pope), 97–111; death in, 107–8; politics in, 99–101; property in, 105–6; retirement in, 98, 101–4, 137

Second Satire of the Second Book of Horace Paraphrased, The (Pope), 77–85, 94, 97, 108, 110

Sellar, W. Y., 54, 125

Shakespeare, William, 115

Sidney, Philip, 58

Sixth Epistle of the First Book of Horace Imitated, The (Pope), 124–28

Sober Advice from Horace (Pope), 85–92, 155 n.20

Spence, Joseph, 30–31, 45, 53

Sporus, 93–96, 155 n.4

Stack, Frank, 135–36, 140, 146 n.3, 153 n.7, 155 n.20, 155–56 n.7, 157 n.14

State of Rome Under Nero and Domitian, The (Whitehead), 20

Steiner, George, 17

Sternhold, Thomas, 120–21, 157 n.15

Strained applications. *See* Application of source meaning: strained

Suetonius, 156 n.11

Swift, Jonathan, 30, 32, 56, 81, 118–19, 127, 140

Tacitus, 29, 36–37

Tiberius, 37, 49, 97

Tigellius, 86–87, 93, 155 n.4

Trapp, Joseph, 47, 151 n.19

Trebatius, 65–76, 158 n.2

Tupper, J. W., 125

Twickenham, 61, 71–76, 78–85, 94–97, 101–2, 121, 123, 137, 140–42

Tytler, Alexander, 17

Vanity of Human Wishes, The (Johnson), 22–26

Vergil, 44–46, 57, 59, 119, 146 n.5, 150 nn. 12 and 13; and Augustus, 46; eighteenth-century reputation of, 29, 38; and Horace, 53–54; idealism of, 54

Walpole, Robert, 73, 124, 140; opposition to, 20, 28–30, 32, 34–36, 48–49, 51, 149 nn. 18 and 20, 149–50 n.21, 157 n.7; Pope on, 59, 131, 141, 144

Warton, Joseph, 44–46, 62, 150 n.12

Watt, Ian, 38, 147–48 n.1, 148 n.3

Weber, Harold, 151 n.18, 154 n.7

Weinbrot, Howard D., 21, 28–30, 34, 35, 38–39, 49, 68, 112, 143, 147 n.1, 156 n.2

Weinsheimer, Joel, 26

Whitehead, Paul, 20

Williams, Aubrey L., 16–17, 99, 153 n.5

Windsor Forest (Pope), 54